Student Support
Materials for
AQA AS Psychology

Unit 2

Biological Psychology, Social Psychology and Individual Differences

Authors: Eleanor Hills and Mike Cardwell
Series editors: Mike Cardwell and Alison Wadeley

Published by Collins Education
An imprint of HarperCollins*Publishers*
77–85 Fulham Palace Road
Hammersmith
London
W6 8JB

Browse the complete Collins Education catalogue at www.collinseducation.com

© HarperCollins*Publishers* Limited 2011
10 9 8 7 6 5 4 3 2 1

ISBN 978-0-00-741840-4

Eleanor Hills and Mike Cardwell assert their moral rights to be identified as the authors of this work.

British Library Cataloguing in Publication Data.
A catalogue record for this publication is available from the British Library.

Commissioned by Charlie Evans and Andrew Campbell
Project managed by Shirley Wakley
Editorial: Hugh Hillyard-Parker
Design and typesetting by G Brasnett, Cambridge
Cover Design by Angela English
Production by Simon Moore
Printed and bound by L.E.G.O. S.p.A. Italy
Indexed by Christine Boylan

Acknowledgements
Every effort has been made to contact the holders of copyright material, but if any have been inadvertently overlooked the publishers will be pleased to make the necessary arrangements at the first opportunity.

Credits and Permissions
p. 5 (Fig. 2), Selye, H. (1956), *The Stress of Life*, New York: McGraw-Hill; p. 8 (Table 2), Holmes, T. & Rahe, R. (1967), 'Holmes-Rahe Social Readjustment Rating Scale', *Journal of Psychosomatic Research*, 11 (2), 213–18, Elsevier Science Ltd; p.14 (Study), Friedman, M. & Rosenman, R. H. (1974), *Type A Behavior and Your Heart*, New York: Knopf; p. 24 (Study), Asch, S. E. (1951), 'Effects of group pressure upon the modification and distortion of judgments', In H. Guetzkow (ed.), *Groups, leadership and men*, 177–90, Pittsburgh, PA: Carnegie Press; p. 25, (Study), Crutchfield, R. (1955), 'Conformity and Character', *American Psychologist*, 10, 191–8, American Psychological Association; p. 25, (Study), Perrin, S. & Spencer, C. (1980), 'The Asch effect – a child of its time', *Bulletin of the British Psychological Society*, 33, 405–6; p. 30–1 (Study), Milgram, S. (1963), 'Behavioral Study of Obedience', *Journal of Abnormal and Social Psychology*, 67 (4), 371–8, Elsevier Science Limited; p.31 (Study), Hofling, C. K. *et al.* (1966), 'An Experimental Study of Nurse–Physician Relationships', *Journal of Nervous and Mental Disease* 143 (2), 171–80, Lippincott, Williams & Wilkins; p. 38 (Fig. 3), adapted from Rotter, J. B. (1954), *Social learning and clinical psychology*, NY: Prentice-Hall; p. 45 (Study), Jahoda, M. (1958), *Current Concepts of Positive Mental Health*, New York: Basic Books; p. 48 (Notes), McGuffin, P., Farmer, A. & Gottesman, I.I. (1987), 'Is there really a split in schizophrenia? The genetic evidence', *The British Journal of Psychiatry*, 150, 581–92, Royal College of Psychiatrists; p. 54 (Table 5), Ellis, A. (1962), *Reason and Emotion in Psychotherapy*, Secaucus, NJ: Lyle Stuart; Beck, A. T. (1967), *Depression: Clinical, Experimental, and Theoretical aspects*, New York: Hoeber; p. 55 (Fig. 5), adapted from Beck, A. T. (1976), *Cognitive Therapy and Emotional Disorders*, New York: International Universities Press; p. 55, (Study), 2004: Rachman, S. (2004), 'Fear of Contamination', *Behaviour Research and Therapy*, 42 (11), 1227–55, Elsevier Science Ltd; p. 56, (Study), Fava, G. A. *et al* (1998), 'Prevention of recurrent depression with cognitive behavioural therapy: preliminary findings', *Archives of General Psychiatry*, 55 (9), 816–20; p. 63, (Fig. 6), Ellis, A. (2001), *Overcoming Destructive Beliefs, Feeling, and Behaviors: New Directions for Rational Emotive Behavior Therapy*, Prometheus Books.

Illustrations and photographs
Cover and p. 1, © Greg Hargreaves/gettyimages.co.uk.

Contents

The body's response to stress

Stress can be defined as:

- the response of an individual to an unpleasant, and potentially threatening, situation
- the response to a stimulus (stressor) in our environment
- a mismatch between perceived demands and our perceived ability to cope with them.

There are two systems that react to stress in the body. One is the reaction to acute (immediate) stress called the **sympathomedullary pathway**; the second is the reaction to chronic stress called the **pituitary–adrenal system**. Figure 1 illustrates the route each system takes through the body.

Both systems are at work as soon as stress occurs, but they have different functions in helping us combat stress.

The sympathomedullary pathway

This system is activated without any conscious control and is vital to our survival. As the stress response is designed to be an adaptive response to a dangerous or threatening situation, this is the system that ensures a speedy and efficient response of the body to escape or tackle the situation.

This pathway involves a higher brain structure called the **hypothalamus**, which acts like a thermostat. Once a need is detected, it alerts the pituitary gland (the 'master gland' located in the brain) and this activates systems that control bodily functions. It does this via the **autonomic nervous system (ANS)**, which has two divisions: the sympathetic and parasympathetic nervous systems.

The sympathetic nervous system (SNS)

This prepares the body for 'fight or flight' (Cannon 1914). Sympathetic arousal causes our heart rate, respiration and blood pressure to increase. Sugars and fatty acids are released into the blood stream to help energize the muscles, and the digestive system is slowed down. The adrenal medulla is stimulated to produce adrenaline (epinephrine) and noradrenaline (norepinephrine), which act as arousal hormones supporting and reinforcing the SNS response.

The parasympathetic nervous system (PNS)

This acts to return the body to a state of normality following a period of sympathetic arousal.

This pathway is very good for immediate and acute stress, but cannot maintain the level of functioning for long. This response is designed to be short-term.

Fig. 1
The routes through the body taken by the two systems involved in the body's stress response

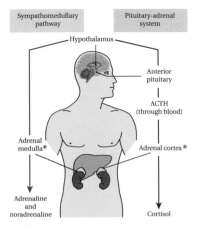

*Essential notes

The adrenal glands are part of the endocrine system, which can release hormones directly into the blood stream. They are located above each kidney. The cortex is the outer layer and the medulla is in the centre (see Fig. 1).

Examiners' notes

The sympathomedullary pathway is outlined in Fig. 1; for 6-mark questions you will need to learn this process.

The pituitary–adrenal system

Unlike the sympathomedullary pathway, the emphasis of this system is not on immediate survival, but on continued energy production. This system is activated by the hypothalamus once a situation is assessed as stressful. It sends corticotrophic releasing factor (CRF) to the pituitary gland, which sends adrenocorticotrophic hormone (ACTH) to the adrenal cortex. This stimulates the release of corticosteroids into the blood stream, which facilitates the release of cortisol (among other hormones) to help the body produce more energy. This system helps the body combat chronic stress by maintaining energy levels. It is designed to work long-term.

Essential notes

It might help you to think of the two systems as athletes. The sympathomedullary pathway is like a sprinter, quick and powerful, while the pituitary–adrenal system is like a marathon runner where the emphasis is on stamina. Table 1 summarizes the two systems.

System	Product	Emphasis of system	Length of activation
Sympathomedullary pathway	Adrenaline and noradrenaline	Speed and strength Survival	Short-term (acute stress)
Pituitary adrenal system	Cortisol	Energy production Stamina	Long-term (chronic stress)

Table 1
Summary of the sympathomedullary and pituitary–adrenal systems

The General Adaptation Syndrome (GAS)

Work by Hans Selye (1956) examined the reaction of the body to chronic stress. Through experiments with rats he discovered a universal physical reaction that occurred over a period of weeks, and he called this the **General Adaptation Syndrome (GAS)**. The reaction fell into three stages, as shown in Fig. 2.

Alarm stage
The pituitary–adrenal system and the sympathomedullary pathway are both activated in the fight or flight response to stress. The hypothalamus stimulates the pituitary gland to produce ACTH in order to bring about the release of corticosteroids from the adrenal cortex. Simultaneously, SNS arousal causes the release of adrenaline and noradrenaline from the adrenal medulla. This enables the body to respond at speed and with energy to the potential problem it faces. This can only be short-term as it is highly demanding of the sympathetic branch of the ANS.

Resistance stage
In this stage, the body does not display outward signs of stress but continues to work hard to maintain energy so that its resistance to stress is maintained as much as possible.

Exhaustion stage
Selye thought that chronic (long-lasting) stress could eventually exhaust hormone reserves so much that the body would be unable to maintain its resistance. At this stage, stress-related illnesses such as high blood pressure, ulcers and mental health problems might manifest themselves.

Phase 1: Alarm

Stress-response – system activated

Phase 2: Resistance

Body copes with stress

Phase 3: Exhaustion

Stress-related illness may develop

Fig. 2
The three stages of Selye's General Adaptation Syndrome

Stress-related illness and the immune system

The immune system

The immune system consists of a complex network of cells and chemicals and protects us against diseases and illnesses. The immune response is triggered by **antigens** – substances that the body recognizes as foreign. Some antigens, such as pollen or house dust, can be harmless to some people but provoke allergic reactions in others. Antigens can also be carried on the surface of harmful disease-causing **pathogens**, such as viruses, bacteria or fungi.

White blood cells, known as lymphocytes and phagocytes, are particularly important in the immune response and protect us in three different ways.

1. **Non-specific immunity**
   Phagocytes, such as macrophages, surround and ingest foreign particles. Macrophages scout for pathogens and alert other macrophages to an invasion when it detects them. They can also alert lymphocytes called helper T cells.

2. **Cell-based immunity**
   T cells, made in the thymus gland, find and destroy cells that they identify as foreign or infected. They activate killer cells known as cytotoxic T cells, which destroy infected cells and activate lymphocytes called B cells.

3. **Antibody-based immunity**
   B cells, made in the bone marrow, attack invading substances in the bloodstream before infections even reach cellular or tissue level. The B cells form plasma cells, which make antibodies that bind to viral antigens and slow them down so that they can be destroyed more easily.

Stress-related illness

Our bodies are designed to react to stress but not for long periods (see the GAS, p. 5). Immune system functioning can be reduced by both acute and chronic stress, although chronic stress is more dangerous.

Acute stress and the immune system

As the acute stress response is designed to be short-term, the immune system should not be dangerously weakened by short periods of stress. However, even short–term stress can cause some problems. In a **natural experiment**, Kiecolt-Glaser *et al.* (1984) monitored T cell activity in the blood of 75 medical students one month before, during and one month after their final exams and found that it was reduced. This means that immune responses could also be reduced, leaving the students more vulnerable to illness.

In evaluating these findings, there are several points to make:
- Medical students might be unlike other students, limiting the generalizability to other groups.

- Kiecolt-Glaser *et al.* (1984, 1991), however, found further support for their conclusions in carers of people with Alzheimer's disease and in women going through divorce.
- Further evidence was provided by Marshall *et al.* (1998), who found that short-term stressors, such as exams, can slow recovery by reducing the production of cytokines, which promote wound healing.
- Acute stress alone may not explain the findings, as it was also found that the presence of co-existing long-term stressors, such as loneliness, could exacerbate the effects of acute stress.

Chronic stress and the immune system

- *Interpersonal conflict* – Cohen (2005) showed that couples in conflict that had lasted for more than a month were especially vulnerable to succumbing to infection when exposed to an infectious agent. Kiecolt-Glaser (2005) supported the idea that immune responses are reduced by showing that blisters on the arms of couples healed more slowly after conflicting discussions compared to after supportive ones. Others, such as Mayne *et al.* (1997), have suggested a gender difference in that women in conflicting couples show stronger immune suppression.
- *Death of a close relative* – Gerra *et al.* (2003) showed lowered natural killer cell and lymphocyte activity in bereaved people compared with matched controls. This difference was still present 40 days after the bereavement and persisted in some individuals for months. Kiecolt-Glaser and Newton (2001) noted a greater effect for widowers.
- *Caregiving* – Kiecolt-Glaser *et al.* (2000) found that long-term care of a dependent relative was associated with lower levels of killer cell activity and poor resistance to viral infection in caregivers compared with matched non-caregivers.

Evaluation of studies of the effect of stress on the immune system

- *Good experimental support* – There are many good-quality, experimental studies (as outlined above) that give clear evidence for changes in immune system to both acute and chronic stress.
- *Reductionism* – To reduce the impact of stress to something that is purely physiological/biological ignores the whole person and the sociocultural context in which they live. Many other factors that are difficult to control in research could be involved, such as depression, anxiety, level of social support and cultural tolerance of weakness.
- *Individual differences* – Some of the studies described above have suggested that variables such as gender might mediate responses to stress. In addition, age or personality factors could make people vary in vulnerability and would need to be controlled if the effects of stress are to be clearly understood. (See discussions of hardiness and Type A/B personality on p. 14.)

Essential notes

Stress is difficult to study because attempts to manipulate it experimentally are ethically challenging. Yet, if it is allowed to occur naturally, many other factors happening in individuals' lives are uncontrolled and can obscure experimental effects.

Essential notes

Kiecolt-Glaser *et al.* (2003) and others have suggested that women respond to marital stress more than men in terms of suppressed immunity. However, men are more susceptible to dying from coronary heart disease (CHD). Taylor *et al.* (2000) have suggested that women have evolved to respond to stress by suppressing the fight or flight urge in order to protect their offspring, while men's SNS is highly activated, putting them at greater risk of high blood pressure and CHD.

Examiners' notes

Questions might be specific on 'stress-related illness and immune system functioning'. Alternatively, questions could ask about stress-related illness *without* specifying the immune system. In such cases, material on other forms of illness (e.g. cardiovascular disease) or mental disorder (e.g. depression) would be relevant. However, if the question restricts you to immune system functioning, this other material would not be creditworthy.

Life changes

Stressors are personal to the individual. Some situations may make some people very stressed, whereas the same thing may not affect someone else to the same extent. However, it is thought there are stressors that prompt the stress reaction in most people – in other words, they are almost universal. There are few things that are certain in life, but one of them is change. Changes happen throughout our lives and although we know they will happen, we sometimes don't react well to them. These so-called **critical life events** are therefore a type of stressor.

The Social Readjustment Rating Scale (SRRS)

Holmes and Rahe's (1967) Social Readjustment Rating Scale (SRRS) is a scale that measures life changes – and hence, to some extent, stress.

The scale was designed by first taking 43 life events generated from 5000 patients' medical records and then asking 400 participants to rate their psychological impact in terms of how much adjustment they would require. Each life event was then assigned an impact value in the form of a life change unit (LCU) score. The top life change on the list was 'Death of a spouse', which had a LCU of 100, whereas the 43rd on the list, 'Minor violation of the law' was assigned a LCU of 11. The list is shown in Table 2. To measure an individual's overall life change score, LCUs are added up for all critical life events experienced in the preceding 12 months.

Examiners' notes

If a question asks for *findings* (e.g. 'What does research on life changes *show*…'), don't spend time describing the SRRS. However, if a question asks for *methods* (e.g. 'How have psychologists investigated…'), then this material becomes relevant.

Table 2
A sample of items from the SRRS showing their rank position and associated LCU score (Holmes and Rahe 1967)

Ranking	Life event	LCU
1	Death of spouse	100
2	Divorce	73
3	Marital separation	65
23	Son or daughter leaving home	29
24	Trouble with in-laws	29
25	Outstanding personal achievement	28
41	Vacation	13
42	Christmas	12
43	Minor violation of the law	11

Research into life changes and stress

Life changes as a source of stress

Rahe *et al.* (1970) wanted to see whether the scores on the SRRS could predict the future onset of illness. A sample of 2500 male American sailors completed the scale to assess how many life events they had experienced in the previous six months. Then, over the following six-month tour of duty, detailed records were kept of each sailor's health status. It was found that there was a positive correlation of +.12 between life change scores and illness scores. It was concluded that, as LCUs were positively correlated with illness scores, experiencing life events predicts the chances of

Essential notes

The positive correlation was small (a perfect positive correlation would be 1.00), but it was statistically significant, i.e. it shows that there was a meaningful relationship between LCUs and health. As LCU scores increased, so did the frequency of illness.

stress-related health breakdown but, since the correlation was not perfect, life events cannot be the only factor contributing to illness.

Desirable and undesirable life events

The impact of undesirable events might be cushioned by the relative frequency of desirable events. To test this, Stone *et al.* (1987) asked married couples to make daily records of life events, including illness, over a period of three months. They found that three to four days prior to illness, desirable events decreased and undesirable events increased, suggesting that the associated stress level had negative health effects.

Divorce and widowhood

Michael and Ben-Zur (2007) studied 130 middle-aged men and women who had been recently divorced or widowed. They found that participants' life satisfaction scores before and after being widowed shifted downwards, but for divorced participants, the shift was upwards. In the latter group, the improvement in life satisfaction might have been due to new and more harmonious partnerships, a trend that was not as clear for widowed participants.

Evaluation of the life changes approach

- *Social desirability bias* – Self-report techniques such as the SRRS are open to bias in that people may want to present themselves in a positive light rather than an accurate one, making their responses untrustworthy.

- *Individual differences in resilience* – The reaction to a life change depends on individual differences. People react differently depending on their personal characteristics. (See pp. 16–17 on hardiness for example.)

- *Correlation not cause* – There is a relationship between life changes and illness supported by the fact that the SRRS predicts illness reasonably accurately; for example, a life change unit total of 299 or more predicts an 80 per cent chance of illness. However, this is not experimental evidence so it cannot be said that life changes cause illness.

- *Perception of life events* – On the SRRS it is assumed that all life change is stressful. This is not always the case; if an event is perceived as positive, then the chances of it actually being stressful are reduced, which should reduce its physical effects.

- *An incomplete account* – The work on daily hassles (see p. 10) illustrates that there are sources of stress other than life changes, so the latter can be seen as a narrow approach to measuring stress. However, life changes are important, so it could be seen as merely an incomplete approach, not an incorrect one.

Examiners' notes
Make sure you can distinguish between *life changes* (which tend to be major transitional events in a person's life) and *daily hassles* (which tend to be relatively minor irritations – see pp. 10–11).

Essential notes
Holmes and Rahe's work was conducted in the 1970s and has been criticized for being out of date and **androcentric**. Nowadays, for example, marriage often follows cohabitation, so the change is minimal to an individual. Items in the SRRS such as 'Wife begins or stops work' clearly do not apply to female respondents.

Daily hassles

One problem with the life changes approach to explaining and measuring stress is that it looks at events that occur relatively infrequently; yet, when asked, people report that short-term, day-to-day problems are also stressful.

Measuring daily hassles (and uplifts)

Essential notes

Further examples of daily hassles include such things as losing something, concerns about weight or appearance, and worries about the health of family members.

Uplifts include sleeping well, eating out and getting along well with others.

Kanner *et al.* (1981) compiled a scale that measures stress based on day-to-day problems, such as having too much to do or being late for something. This is known as the Hassles Scale. It measures stress by working on the theory that the more daily hassles you encounter in life, the more stressful it seems.

Daily life is not necessarily always a struggle. We also experience pleasant everyday occurrences that could lessen stress. For this reason, the scale was further developed to take into account uplifts. An example is that, although the daily practicalities of bringing up children can be stressful hassles, these can be offset by the rewarding aspects of parenting.

Why are daily hassles stressful?

Daily hassles erode our coping resources
Many researchers think that daily hassles are a better explanation of stress than the relatively infrequent life changing events measured by the SRRS. The effect of relatively minor but persistent stressors accumulates over time and thus makes any further hassles more stressful because our ability to cope is depleted. This could result in more serious conditions such as anxiety disorders and/or depression (Lazarus 1999).

Daily hassles are amplified by existing chronic stressors
An alternative viewpoint reverses the pathway of events by proposing that the presence of more serious chronic stressors may in themselves create hassles, but also make other daily hassles seem more serious than they really are. For example, breaking a leg and having to use crutches to get around (rated 6th on the SRRS for being life-changing) causes everyday practical difficulties but may make missing a bus more frustrating than normal.

Examiners' notes

When using research as AO2 evaluation, make sure you set it in the context of a critical commentary rather than just describing a study and hoping for the best. An examiner will not assume that you know *why* a particular study is important in evaluating a theory or idea; you need to make this explicit.

Research supporting the daily hassles approach

Daily hassles and nursing
Gervais (2005) asked nurses to keep diaries for a month describing job-related daily hassles and uplifts, as well as recording how they felt they were performing in their jobs. It was found that uplifts usually served to cancel out hassles and were related to improved job performance and lowered stress levels, suggesting that both daily hassles and uplifts contributed to stress levels.

Daily hassles and students' transition to university

Bouteyre *et al.* (2007) tested 233 French, first-year psychology students using a depression inventory and the Hassles Scale. It was found that, during the initial transition from school to university, 41 per cent of students had depressive symptoms and that hassles scores correlated positively with these. Transition to university can be thought of as a life-changing, critical event, but it also comes with many hassles, such as money worries and feeling lonely, stressors which could contribute to depression.

Daily hassles and illness

Delonghis *et al.* (1982) found that the Hassles Scale predicted illness well. Indeed, when compared to the relationship between life changes and illness, it was found that the Hassles Scale was superior. This is surprising given the magnitude of some of the events, so perhaps everyday stress has a greater effect on us than we perceive it does. It seems, however, that daily uplifts are not as closely linked to illness as are hassles. Their effect is probably more to moderate (or reduce) the effect of the hassles rather than to function independently.

Evaluation of the daily hassles approach

Cultural differences

Kim and McKenry (1998) found that there are cultural differences in the extent of social support available to individuals from family, friends and religious groups. Such support was found to be greater with African Americans and Asian Americans compared to Caucasians, and was associated with lowered stress in difficult situations, such as caring for a relative with Alzheimer's disease. If someone is well supported by significant others, such as family and friends, any stressor should have less effect. In this case, support appeared to be associated with less stress from daily hassles, which accords with the predictions derived from this approach.

Correlation vs cause

As with the SRRS, there is a distinction between saying that daily hassles *predict* illness levels and that they actually *cause* them. There are many other factors that can influence mental and physical health in addition to daily hassles. However, we do know that daily hassles can be acute stressors, and these trigger the body's fight or flight response, so there is a physiological/biological reaction even if it is short lived. (See pp. 4–5 for the body's reaction to acute stress.) If this happens repeatedly, it could weaken resistance to further stress, as Lazarus (1999) suggested.

Examiners' notes

Research that supports psychologists' theories can always be used in examination answers to elaborate on evaluations. For example, for this topic you might write: 'Research has shown that the daily hassles approach to predicting stress is a valid one. For example, Gervais (2005) found that... and concluded that...'. (See p. 66 for more information on how to elaborate your answers.)

Essential notes

Caring for a relative with long-term illness is a chronic stressor and causes many daily hassles. Kim and McKenry's research suggests that social support can somehow ameliorate the effects of both.

Essential notes

The Health and Safety at Work Act states that both employers and employees have legal rights and responsibilities towards each other in the workplace – for example, the employer must carry out regular risk assessments, and employees must report any conditions that adversely affect them to enable the employer to make changes.

Essential notes

Recent decades have seen a rise in the number of dual-career families and a corresponding increase in stress caused by parents attempting to juggle both work and family responsibilities (ten Brummelhuis *et al.* 2010).

Essential notes

The phrase 'lunch is for wimps' crept into common usage in the 1980s when long hours and competition in the workplace discouraged employees from taking rest breaks. Hill (2008) reported that only 16 per cent of British employees take a regular lunch break and that the average break is just 27 minutes.

Workplace stress

According to government sources (www.directgov.co.uk 2011), one in five employees suffers from work-based stress. The Health and Safety at Work Act (1974) states that employers have a duty of care towards their employees to enable them to perform well and be productive in their work without being unduly stressed or succumbing to stress-related illness. Psychological research can help both employers and employees understand the sources and effects of workplace stress so that they can deal with it effectively. Failure to address workplace stress could lead to physical and mental exhaustion – a condition that Maslach (1982) called **burnout**.

Stress arises from a number of aspects of working life, including work overload, job control and role ambiguity.

Work overload

Britain is regarded as the workaholic of Europe because there is a culture of working longer and longer hours. There are several reasons for work overload:

- It is simply expected.
- It becomes linked to success and self-esteem.
- During recession, employees take on the work of those who have lost their jobs, fearing that if they do not, they may also be laid off.
- The globalization of working practices means that, in order to survive, businesses need to be available round the clock so that they can work with different time zones.

There is much research demonstrating the damaging effects of work overload. For example, Dewe (1992) found that excessive workload is one of the greatest sources of stress in the workplace. It increases the amount of time spent at work, diminishes opportunities to escape and relax, and has detrimental effects on family and social life.

A question of balance

Scultz *et al.* (2010) used data from a survey of 16 000 workers in the USA and found that, as expected, work overload was associated with a higher proportion of reported negative health outcomes. However, they also showed that work underload, where workers felt bored and insufficiently valued or challenged, was almost as damaging. The least affected workers were those whose workload matched their expectations. This demonstrates that:

- work overload is associated with poorer health
- how the worker perceives their workload could influence how well they cope.

Lack of control

Seligman and Maier (1967) demonstrated that, when dogs were given a series of inescapable electric shocks, they would not subsequently take opportunities to escape. They called this behaviour **learned helplessness** and suggested that humans unable to control what happened to them could experience a similar state, which could lead to depression.

Stress in Whitehall civil servants

Marmot *et al.* (1991) carried out a three-year longitudinal study of over 3000 civil servants. Those with low autonomy (control) in their work were four times more likely to die of a heart attack than those with high autonomy. This negative correlation was also apparent in a review of the effects of highly demanding jobs with little control (Van der Doef and Maes 1998), suggesting that low control is a stressor that could contribute to poor health.

Locus of control

While the degree of control a person has in the workplace can be an objective fact, individual differences in **locus of control (LOC)** (Rotter 1954) may contribute to its effects. People with internal LOC tend to feel responsible for events in their lives, while externalizers blame outside influences. In the workplace, Gray Stanley *et al.* (2010) showed that a tendency to internal LOC moderated the effects of work overload, suggesting that the way in which individuals construe control can have practical consequences for their health.

Unwelcome control

A high level of control can be a source of stress for certain individuals. Schaubroeck *et al.* (2001) studied a wide range of occupations, such as building maintenance and data analysis, and found that people who felt that they could meet the demands of their jobs, and felt responsible when things went wrong, suffered the most stress. They showed lower levels in their saliva of IgA antibodies, which fight upper respiratory infection from bacteria or viruses, making them more susceptible to colds and flu. This correlation suggests that feeling overstretched by too much responsibility can be as stressful as having too little control and lead to negative health outcomes.

Evaluation

Correlation vs causality

While the association between stress and mental and physical health problems is well established, much of the research is correlational. This is partly because it would be unethical to manipulate workplace stressors experimentally in order to observe their effects. The exact nature of the association therefore remains open to conjecture.

Individual differences

Individual differences such as age, gender, culture, cognition and personality (see pp. 14–17 on Type A/B behaviour and hardiness) all affect how people react to stress. They also help to explain why some people thrive in a workplace while others are unaffected or become ill. It is difficult for researchers to control for all of these known variables and hence understand fully the impact of workplace stress.

Examiners' notes

Questions may also require you to apply your psychological knowledge of this area in a novel situation (e.g. recognizing workplace stressors and offering advice as to how a particular workplace could be made less stressful).

Essential notes

The trustworthiness of workplace stress research may be affected by people:
- not wanting to reveal how stressed they feel for fear of appearing weak or losing their job
- not having sufficient clarity of insight to realize how much stress they are under.

Personality factors and stress: Type A and Type B behaviour

Personality has been shown to be one of many factors associated with the effect of potential stressors. Three key concepts in this area are Type A and Type B behaviour, and hardiness (see pp. 16–17).

Type A and Type B behaviour

Two cardiologists, Friedman and Rosenman (1974), carried out an 8½-year longitudinal study of 3200 healthy Californian men aged 39 to 59 and identified a constellation of 'hurry-sickness' tendencies, which they called **Type A behaviour**. They described it as '…an action-emotion complex that can be observed in any person who is aggressively involved in a chronic, incessant struggle to achieve more and more in less and less time, and if required to do so, against the opposing efforts of other things or other persons.' (Further examples of Type A behaviour are shown in Table 3.)

Behavioural type was assessed by carrying out structured interviews about typical behaviour patterns, e.g. when in a queue or driving, and by monitoring behaviour such as impatience and hostility during the interview. Friedman and Rosenman also named the absence of Type A behaviour **Type B behaviour**. People in this category were more relaxed about events generally, more patient and had a more positive outlook on life; they also had lower levels of stress and a lower associated incidence of CHD (coronary heart disease). Later, Friedman and Rosenman also named unclassified individuals as Type AB.

Over the duration of the study, 257 men developed CHD, and 70 per cent of these were Type A while 30 per cent were not. It was concluded that Type A behaviour may lead to a more stressful lifestyle and a greater susceptibility to stress-related illnesses such as CHD.

Evaluation of Type A and B behaviour research

Any research showing that reaction to stress is associated with behaviour patterns supports the idea that the distinction between Type A and Type B behaviour is a valid one. Friedman and Rosenman's work has inspired many more researchers.

Refining the concept of Type

A review of studies by Hemingway (1999) found that development of CHD and the hostility element of Type A personality seemed to be linked, suggesting that just one personality attribute rather than personality type may affect stress.

Williams *et al.* (2003) also examined the different components that make up Type A behaviour and found that higher levels of hostility and impatience increased the risk of hypertension (high blood pressure), which is associated with CHD and strokes. Research such as this helps to refine understanding of Type and make treatment more focused.

Table 3
Type A behaviour pattern

Time pressure
• Working against the clock • Doing several things at once • Irritation and impatience with others • Unhappy doing nothing
Competitive
• Always playing to win at games and at work • Achievement measured as material productivity
Anger
• Self-critical • Hostile to the outside world • Anger often directed inwards

Essential notes

The Jenkins Activity Survey was developed to identify behavioural type. Later versions of it sorted people into A1 (Type A), A2 (not completely Type A), Type AB (a balance of Types A and B) and B (completely or almost completely Type B).

Evidence for physiological/biological differences

Recently, there has been renewed research interest in possible physiological/biological differences between Type A and B personalities.

- Rebollo and Boomsma (2006) measured Type A behaviour in 1760 parents with identical (MZ) or fraternal (DZ) twins. They used statistical techniques to show that 45 per cent of the variation in Type A behaviour was attributable to genetics.

- Konareva (2011) reported that patterns of **EEG (electroencephalography)** activity differ between individuals with Type A and either Type B or AB behaviour. EEG activity depends on inherited, neurochemical factors, which could influence a person's disposition.

Both these studies suggest a genetic contribution to Type. There is not much that can be done to change genes themselves, but understanding the extent of their contribution helps to clarify the best treatment. For example, drug treatments for stressed Type A people might be the only practical option.

Applicability across genders

Friedman and Rosenman's work used only male participants, raising the question of whether women are similar. Changes in women's working patterns since the 1960s have exposed them more to similar workplace stresses, which may help explain why in the UK the gap in CHD is closing, although CHD remains more common in men (NHS 2011). In addition, women stereotypically have closer, more supportive relationships with others, which should help to buffer stress. Vroege and Aaronson (1994), however, found that fewer Type A employed men or women tended to seek social support than did Type B people. The link with CHD might therefore be explained by both lack of social support and Type A behaviour in both sexes.

Practical aspects of research into Type A and Type B behaviour

Correlational studies

Prospective, longitudinal studies help to control for individual differences and can show clear correlations between Type and disease. However, it is unethical to manipulate stress levels to observe their effect, so we cannot be sure whether personality type causes stress-related health problems. In fact, personality type may be one reason why people initially seek particular occupations.

Consistency of personality

The Type A/B approach assumes that personality remains relatively stable. However, Mischel (1968) has proposed that how we behave is determined by our situation, and consistency is an illusion resulting from encountering ourselves and others in a limited range of contexts. If Mischel is correct, the entire basis of the Type A/B approach is flawed.

Examiners' notes

In order to answer specific exam questions, you will need to précis the material on these two pages. Check through the question types described on p. 68 and practise adjusting the material to suit every type of question.

Essential notes

Remember there are many other factors that affect the development of CHD – such as diet, smoking, high blood pressure, high cholesterol and physical fitness – and all these need to be considered when assessing the validity of research findings.

Personality factors and stress: hardiness

Research considered so far in this chapter suggests that our reactions to stressors are determined by a complex interplay of different variables. To name just a few, these include Type A and B personality, social support, locus of control, culture and gender. Such variables go some way to explaining differences in what people perceive as stressful, but they do not fully account for why some individuals are more susceptible to stress than others.

The hardy personality

Essential notes

The stress-hardy personality is characterized by a positive attitude to the three Cs:
● control
● commitment
● challenge.

Examiners' notes

Try this exam preparation task. Construct:

(a) a 2-mark explanation of hardiness

(b) a 3-mark outline of the link between hardiness and stress (50 to 75 words)

(c) a 6-mark description of the link between hardiness and stress (120 to 150 words)

(d) two 3-mark critical points relating to the link between hardiness and stress (120 to 150 words in total)

(e) a 12-mark essay outlining and evaluating the link between hardiness and stress (300 to 350 words).

Note: The final task (e) might appear to be just a case of linking together (c) and (d), but 12-mark essay questions require a little more for both AO1 and AO2, so add about 50 words more elaboration to each of your (c) and (d) answers and you may have a first-rate essay for this area!

Kobasa (Kobasa and Maddi 1977) found that there were certain individuals who seemed to be generally better equipped than others to resist the effects of stress. She described them as having a **hardy personality**, and claimed that this consists of three key factors that help keep stress at a minimum:

● *Control* – The individual has an internal LOC (see p. 13): they feel they are in control of what happens to them rather than feeling they are a victim of circumstances.

● *Commitment* – The individual gets involved in life and engages with those around them. This means they are less likely to give up when the going gets tough, especially if they have gathered social support around themselves.

● *Challenge* – The hardy individual seems to appraise situations in a different way to others, seeing any changes in life as a positive challenge. This leaves them less vulnerable to stressful feelings of being unable to cope.

Hardiness emphasizes that being in control is important to reduce stress levels. There is research evidence to support this argument. However, the role of control is not always clear. If someone feels they have to be totally in control, they may have associated issues that can lead to obsessive behaviour, which then raises the levels of anxiety. This makes the relationship complicated.

Evaluation of hardy personality research

Evidence in favour of hardiness

Kobasa *et al.* (1985) carried out a prospective longitudinal study, which she began by measuring participants' hardiness, social support and exercise, all of which she thought were protective against stress. She then followed up the participants to assess their psychological and physical health. Those with no protective factors had the highest scores on severity of illness scales, while illness progressively decreased with the addition for one, two and three factors, suggesting that these acted in a cumulative way. Hardiness, however, had the most effect, lending validity to the idea that it protects against stress.

Sample bias

Much of Kobasa's work was conducted on professional men, which means that there is an androcentric sample bias in her work. This does not mean that she is wrong, but that generalizing to both genders and cross culturally is problematic. It might mean that being hardy reduces stress to a greater extent for men only.

Distinction between factors

Control, commitment and challenge have not been defined exactly, neither has how they work together. It may be that:

- only one of those is the key factor to reducing stress (control is the most likely), or
- they vary in importance, or
- they operate in a linear fashion, e.g. people with internal LOC only commit to things they think they can manage and so they see it as a challenge, or
- they work together synergistically, such that their combined effect is more powerful than simply adding their individual contributions together.

Practical applications to stress management: hardiness training

Kobasa's work has led her to develop a stress management programme in which an individual can learn to become hardy. It is a three-stage process that involves:

- *Focusing* – The individual is able to notice their stressors.
- *Reliving stressful encounters* – The client would think about recent stressful situations and how they could have been dealt with differently to reduce the level of stress experienced.
- *Self-improvement* – The stage in which an individual learns to avoid stress in the future by thinking about and appraising potentially stressful situations differently. This invariably means that they need to feel in control and see problems as a challenge rather than as overwhelming.

Hardiness is determined by measuring the three variables separately, so in theory, the focus of training can be adapted to work on the weakest one. The fact that this programme is successful for some highly committed and motivated individuals highlights the effect that hardiness and, more generally, personality may have on the individual's experience of stress. However, it is also true that the success of a treatment does not necessarily mean that the theory behind it is sound. Improvements might come about for other reasons, such as the beneficial effect of the care and attention someone else gives to your welfare, or it may even be a **placebo effect** – it only works because you believe it will.

Essential notes

This is a similar evaluation point to the reference to hostility and stress in Type A behaviour (see 'Evaluation of Type A and B behaviour research' on p. 14). Some components of it might be more influential than others, so it would be reasonable to think in this way for hardiness too.

Essential notes

A placebo effect is any improvement in health or behaviour that is not directly attributable to medication or treatment. Placebos are commonly used in the testing of drugs, where it is possible that simply receiving *any* medication (even if it has no physiological effect) makes the patient feel more confident that they will recover. By extension, the same would be true of psychological therapies; the patient feels more valued, has more hope of recovery and benefits from the attention they are receiving rather than any quality of the particular form of therapy they are receiving.

Physiological/biological methods of stress management

Drug therapy

Physiological methods manage the effects of stress on the body; they are biologically based. The most widely used physiological/biological method is drug therapy, and there are two main types of drugs used: benzodiazepines and beta blockers.

Benzodiazepines

Benzodiazepines (BZs), such as Valium (diazepam) and Librium, are an effective method to calm down the body when stressed. They work by reducing the arousal level of the brain. This happens by BZs encouraging the action of a chemical in the brain called GABA (gamma-aminobutyric acid). GABA's function is to stop other brain chemicals exciting the neurons and so when someone takes BZs, the level of excitation in their brain decreases. They have a sedative effect, making the person feel calmer.

Beta blockers

An example of a beta blocker is Inderal. Unlike BZs, beta blockers do not work on the brain chemicals. Instead they calm the body by affecting the sympathetic nervous system (see pp. 4–5). Stress arouses this system, increasing the heart and blood pressure. Beta blockers reverse that increase, slowing the heart rate and lowering the blood pressure. The beta blockers work in the blood, preventing cells from receiving the message to respond to stress. Essentially, they block the message, hence their name. Beta blockers, like BZs make the individual feel calmer.

Biofeedback: an alternative physiological/biological method

This technique, like beta blockers, calms the sympathetic nervous system (SNS), but does it in a non-biochemical way. The person is first taught relaxation techniques, such as meditation, then a monitor feeds back physiological signs of SNS arousal to the individual, e.g. heart rate or blood pressure. When there is a significant increase in the heart rate, the monitor alerts the person by a light coming on, a buzzer or a vibrating alarm. They should then use the relaxation technique to calm themselves down.

The fact that the situation alerts the person to their stress levels means that it also helps them to highlight the source of stress. This is always useful in stress management. However, it is thought that it is actually the relaxation technique that is the beneficial part of the biofeedback therapy and so perhaps the machine is not always necessary.

Evaluation of physiological/biological methods of stress management

Emotion-focused approach

Drug therapy is an emotion-focused approach to managing stress. It tackles the arousal in the body, but not the stressor itself. This means that, although the person can feel calmer, there is a possibility that the problems may return if they stop taking the drugs. It can be argued, therefore, that this is only a temporary measure, and more long-term solutions such as SIT (see p. 20), which is a problem-focused approach, may be better.

Biofeedback is also an emotion-focused approach, but differs from drug therapy in that it helps to identify the stressor. By recognizing when arousal levels increase, the individual can learn the kind of situations (or people!) that cause them stress. While this still doesn't prevent the problem reoccurring, it does mean that the individual has a better informed approach to managing stress than drug therapy gives them.

Side effects

All drugs have side effects, so a decision has to be made about whether these outweigh the benefits. BZs have a sedative effect, so drowsiness can be a common side effect. This also decreases alertness and concentration, affecting an individual's ability to drive, work and think clearly. In rare cases, liver functioning can be affected.

Beta blockers have fewer side effects than BZs. However, the action of the drug slows the heart rate and lowers blood pressure, which causes dizziness, and cold hands and feet.

Biofeedback may be a better alternative, as it is reliant on individuals relaxing themselves and does not have side effects.

Tolerance

If BZs are taken for a prolonged period of time, **tolerance** for the drug can develop. This means that the body gets used to the drug so an increased amount is needed to have the desired effect, and addiction may become a risk.

Although beta blockers are not susceptible to tolerance problems in the same way as BZs, there are still long-term issues. The risk of developing Type 2 diabetes increases with prolonged use (NICE 2006); also there can be problems with breathing, as the drug narrows the airways. Biofeedback, therefore, may be a better long-term way of managing stress.

Speed of effectiveness

The speed with which BZs and beta blockers work means that they are a popular method for managing acute stress or in an unexpected situation. Biofeedback acts much more slowly initially as the individual has to learn to make it work. However, once trained, biofeedback can also reduce physical arousal quickly. Many would argue, however, that there would be times when the stress is very sudden and very serious, when drugs are the only really effective method.

Examiners' notes

Even though it is enough to know both drug types, it is helpful to know one physiological/biological alternative to drug therapy to enhance any evaluation on a 12-mark question. Biofeedback provides that alternative.

Examiners' notes

You will probably use the biofeedback technique as a means to evaluate the other ways of managing stress, particularly drug therapy. As an example of a contrasting approach you will need an understanding of what it is and how it works, not lots of detail. Please remember that drug therapy is stated on the specification, so can be asked for specifically in an exam question. Biofeedback is not named, so is a supplementary stress management method.

Essential notes

A general criticism of drug treatments for psychological conditions is that they are reductionist and do not treat the whole person or the source of the problem. They can, however, calm a person sufficiently to allow them to address the problem in other ways.

Psychological methods of stress management

Stress inoculation training (SIT)

SIT was developed by Meichenbaum and Cameron (1983) and is designed to change the way the individual thinks and behaves in potentially stressful situations. It is therefore a cognitive–behavioural therapy, tackling stress by changing the way someone appraises a situation, ensuring that the situation is seen as less stressful. It is a three-stage process conducted over a period of time.

1. Conceptualization

Conceptualization tackles the thinking (or cognitive) component. The therapist asks the client to talk about previously stressful situations and how they felt (e.g. overwhelmed with work). The therapist also asks them to analyse what they were thinking and why, so the client starts to understand themselves better. For example: a client may talk about how they panicked in an exam. With encouragement from the therapist, the client talks about being underprepared and not covering all the topics.

2. Skills training and practice

This stage is designed to ensure that the client has the necessary skills to deal with their stress, and is often personalized, as stressors are personal. Clients are taught general methods of reducing stress (emotion-focused approaches), such as relaxation techniques, as well as more specific techniques that relate to the individual and their stressors. These could be social skills, organizational skills or mediation skills. For example: someone who finds exams stressful may be taught how to relax in the exam room (general skills), as well as techniques for organizing revision (specific skills).

3. Real-life application

The third stage is putting the skills into practice. Contact is maintained with the therapist throughout and follow-up sessions occur so that the individual continues to feel supported in combating their stress. For example: the client plans a revision timetable and uses relaxation techniques in the exam.

Progressive muscle relaxation (PMR)

PMR is a psychological technique for stress management, but works on the body to lower the level of arousal brought about by the stress response. Muscle tension is a common response to stress and this technique aims to reduce it and, in turn, reduce heart rate and blood pressure. The person is taught to concentrate on relaxing each muscle group in the body in turn until they are fully relaxed, and encouraged to check that they are maintaining relaxation in all muscles while moving from one muscle group to the next. The end result is a marked reduction in tension in the body, which reduces the effects of stress and, for some, clears the mind. Essentially, though, this is an emotion-focused approach.

Evaluation of psychological methods

Problem-focused or emotion-focused approach?

SIT is a problem-focused approach as it attempts to deal with stressors and prevent their reoccurrence so that stress is not experienced at all. On the other hand, PMR is used when the stressor occurs, i.e. the stress *is* experienced. PMR is, therefore, an emotion-focused approach and, unlike SIT, does not prevent stress. See pp. 22–3 for more about problem-focused and emotion-focused approaches.

Side effects and tolerance

Unlike drug treatments, there are only beneficial physical side effects and no long-term risks to these methods. Tolerance is only an issue for drug treatments; with psychological methods, there is nothing for the body to get used to. There may be financial effects – e.g. paying for training – and time needed to train. Both SIT and PMR train people to use techniques that can actually reduce stress levels in the long term.

Speed of effectiveness

Initially, these methods require so much training that, unlike drug treatments, they do not work quickly enough in an acutely stressful situation. However, once the skills to relax and deal with a stressful situation have been learnt, they can be used relatively speedily in an acutely stressful situation.

Availability

Training is available to most people in the UK for both these methods, if someone wants it. However, it would be costly unless prescribed as a treatment by a doctor, so it may not be equally available to everyone.

Problems for individuals

These methods require the individual to work hard on reducing their stress. Training can only inform someone of what they have to do, so some people may have difficulty finding the time, or inclination, to make them work. SIT, as a problem-focused approach, requires a lot of time and effort to prevent the stress entirely. As it is essentially trying to change the individual's personality, it can be very difficult. Motivation is an issue with SIT and it does not suit everyone. Indeed, for some, the need to practise can itself put pressure on the individual and so become a stressor.

Table 4

A summary of the two physiological/biological and two psychological approaches to stress management

Key evaluation point	Drug therapy	Biofeedback	SIT (a form of CBT)	PMR
Problem- or emotion-focused?	Emotion	Emotion	Problem	Emotion
Side effects/ tolerance	A risk	None	None	None
Long-term issues	Health issues	None	Beneficial long-term	Beneficial long-term
Speed of effectiveness	Very fast	Fast, once learnt	Fast, once learnt	Fast, once learnt
Availability	Via doctor	Via trainer	Via trainer	Via trainer

Emotion-focused and problem-focused coping

Research by Folkman and Lazarus (1980) into how people cope with stress found that coping strategies fall into two main types. These are emotion-focused and problem-focused strategies and are used in combination or on their own, depending on the person and/or the stressor.

Emotion-focused strategies

These concentrate on calming the subjectively experienced feelings of stress and reducing its effect on the body. An example would be to take a relaxing bath, seek social support (get help from friends or family) or go for a run. Emotion-focused strategies are therefore often seen as a cure for stress rather than prevention.

Problem-focused strategies

These are methods that deal with the stress before it happens, or prevent it from occurring again. Examples are making a revision timetable to manage time when approaching an exam or researching a health issue to ensure decision-making is well informed. These strategies are designed to prevent stress rather than cure it.

Choosing a strategy

The strategy that an individual chooses varies a great deal, influenced by both individual differences and preferences, and situational factors:

- *Resources* – Opportunities to research treatment options in detail may be limited, e.g. no internet access.
- *Personality* – An individual's personality will affect their preferred style, e.g. they may be Type A.
- *Problem-solving ability* – A lack of problem-solving ability would reduce the chance of using a problem-focused strategy, e.g. if the situation were completely novel.
- *Event type* – There may be no time to use a problem-focused strategy, so an emotion-focused one is the only option, e.g. in an emergency, panic must be dealt with first.

Research into emotion- and problem-focused strategies

The influence of controllability

Park *et al.* (2004) asked undergraduates to describe their most recently experienced stressful event, how controllable it was, how they dealt with it and their daily mood. The more problem-focused students reported a more positive mood but only when dealing with controllable stressors.

Fang *et al.* (2006), however, found that, among women who were genetically at higher risk of developing ovarian cancer, problem-focused coping was associated with greater distress over time. This was probably because, knowing they were at risk, they constantly thought about it but worried because they could do nothing to prevent the disease. In this case, being watchful for symptoms but using emotion-focused coping might have been a better strategy.

Evaluation of emotion- and problem-focused strategies

Measurement of different coping styles is problematic

Coping styles can be measured in the 'Ways of Coping Questionnaire' (Folkman and Lazarus 1988) but this contains items that could be seen as both emotion- and problem-focused. For example, responding to stress by 'talking to someone about a problem' could be both emotion-focused (to cheer you up after a stressful situation) or problem-focused (discussing ways to stop the stress). This affects the validity of the measure and any research based on it.

Emotion-focused strategies can have associated problems

Research suggests that some emotion-focused strategies exacerbate health problems (Penley *et al* 2002), such as an increased chance of depression. It is difficult to know, however, if this is because people with a predisposition to depression choose emotion-focused approaches or suffer from depression because they tend to use emotion-focused approaches.

Problem-focused strategies can have associated problems

Problem-focused strategies are also not without their problems. If a stressor is a threat then it is necessary to use emotion-focused strategies first before a problem-focused approach can be employed (Rukholm and Viverais 1993). As emotion-focused strategies calm the physical effects of stress, the arousal level drops so that the individual can think more clearly and solve the problem. If anxiety levels are too high, then problem-solving ability diminishes. It is also useful to recognize feelings and emotions prior to dealing with a problem, so problem-solving strategies alone may not be a good idea.

Gender differences

When women use emotion-focused strategies, they tend to choose ones which concern how they feel (such as 'having a good cry'), whereas men tend to use emotion-focused strategies that distract from the problem, such as going out for a drink or playing sport. This difference seems to be linked to a higher incidence of lower mood in women than men, although this cannot be said to be causal.

There seems to be a bias towards men using problem-focused strategies and women using emotion-focused strategies (Brody and Hall 1993). However, this can depend on what job the individual does (Rosario 1988). Women are also more likely to use social support (Rosario 1988) but it is the way in which this is used that dictates whether it is emotion-focused or problem-focused (see 'Measurement of different coping styles is problematic' above).

Essential notes

What is the difference between problem-focused and emotion-focused approaches to coping? A problem-focused approach to coping would involve dealing directly with the source of stress (e.g. trying to find a constructive solution), whereas an emotion-focused approach would involve dealing with the negative emotions associated with the stress resulting from this stressor.

Examiners' notes

When two evaluation points overlap, as here with the gender differences and problematic measurement of different coping styles, then try to ensure you use them together when answering a 12-mark question. This will mean that your evaluation flows better and sounds less like a list of evaluation points.

Conformity (majority influence)

Social influence refers to the process by which an individual's attitudes, beliefs or behaviours are modified by the presence or actions of others.

Conformity is the process of yielding to **majority influence** and is defined by Myers (1999) as 'a change in behaviour or belief as a result of real or imagined group pressure'. The most influential studies carried out in this area were by Solomon Asch in the 1950s.

Asch (1951)

Asch (1951) was interested in whether individuals would yield to a unanimous majority on a perceptual judgement task, even when the correct answers were always obvious.

Asch's methodology

Asch recruited male student volunteers who were first given a **cover story** that they were to take part in a vision test. Participants were seated around a table and shown a standard line and three comparison lines. Their task was to state out loud which of the comparison lines was the same length as the standard line. Six of the participants were **confederates** of the experimenter and one was a '**naïve' participant**, who always answered second to last. There were 18 trials in the study, and on 12 of these, the confederates unanimously gave the same wrong answer.

The real aim of the study was to see how the naïve participants reacted to the behaviour of these confederates. In subsequent experimental manipulations, Asch varied the size of the group, the unanimity of the majority and so on to investigate the effect of situational variables on the level of conformity.

Asch's findings

On the 12 trials where the confederates gave the same wrong answer, the naïve participant conformed (i.e. gave the same wrong answer as the majority) 36.7 per cent of the time, with 74 per cent of the participants conforming at least once. When participants gave their responses in private, they were right 99 per cent of the time. The majority of participants who did conform admitted that they had gone along with the majority to avoid ridicule (**normative social influence**, see p. 28).

In Asch's variations, he found that when the majority consisted of only two people, the conformity rate dropped to 12.8 per cent. However, majority sizes of more than three did not result in significant increases in conformity above the figure found in the main study. Asch also found that levels of conformity dropped dramatically (to just 5 per cent) when one confederate gave the same answer as the naïve participant.

Examiners' notes

Although it is tempting to describe Asch's study as an experiment, it is not, because the dependent variable (the level of conformity) was not a direct consequence of any independent variable manipulated by the experimenter. We could describe Asch's variations as experimental in that he varied different aspects of the study (such as group size) to assess their impact on conformity levels.

Examiners' notes

Many different percentages are quoted for Asch's study of conformity as Asch carried out three studies using students from three different institutions. With a majority of six confederates, the average level of conformity across these three different samples was 36.72 per cent. With a majority of just three confederates, it was close to 32 per cent. In your answers you can give approximate percentages for these. Note that this was not the percentage of participants who conformed; it was the percentage of the 'critical' trials (where the confederates gave the same wrong answer) that produced a conforming response in the naïve participant.

Other research on conformity

Crutchfield (1955)

Crutchfield believed that the conformity found by Asch might have resulted from participants interacting with each other face to face. He arranged participants in separate booths. Participants had to press a button to give their decision after they saw what they believed were the judgements of the other participants on the screen in front of them (although the experimenter actually controlled these 'judgements' and all participants were shown the same information). Despite the absence of a face-to-face group, conformity levels were 30 per cent when using an Asch-type task, and rose when the task was made more difficult.

Perrin and Spencer (1980)

Perrin and Spencer (1980, 1981) replicated Asch's original study, using British students. When using maths, science and engineering students (who would not have heard of the '**Asch effect**'), they found only one conforming response in 396 trials. However, when participants and settings were selected so that the personal costs of not yielding to the majority would be high, they achieved levels of conformity similar to those found by Asch. This included using youths on probation as participants with probation officers as the majority.

Perrin and Spencer also achieved levels of conformity similar to Asch when the participants were alienated unemployed Black youths with a majority of black confederates and a White experimenter.

Types of conformity

Compliance

Compliance is publicly conforming to the views or behaviours of the majority (to gain approval or avoid disapproval) while privately maintaining one's own views. Compliance tends to be a consequence of normative social influence. People in groups engage in social comparison, watching others' behaviour, then adjusting their own behaviour to fit in (e.g. making a conscious decision to agree with their peer group because group approval is more important than stating their own views).

Internalization

Internalization is changing private views to match those of the group. When exposed to the views of others, people engage in a validation process, examining the views of the majority against their own in order to see who is right. After closely examining the group position (if different to their own), they may decide that they are wrong and the group is right.

Internalization tends to be a consequence of **informational social influence** (see p. 29). Internalization leads to acceptance of the group's point of view, and a change of private attitude rather than just public compliance (e.g. a person changing their attitude because they believe others have greater expertise).

(see p. 29)

Examiners' notes

You could use Perrin and Spencer's research to make an evaluative point, i.e. that Asch's results were largely due to the perceived pressures to conform at the time of **McCarthyism** in the USA, and the potential costs of standing out.

Examiners' notes

Remember that appropriate examples of these types of conformity are useful as a way of elaborating your explanation, but should not be used instead of explaining conformity.

Essential notes

A third 'type' of conformity is identification – adopting the views or behaviours of a group both publicly and privately because the individual values membership of that group. However, these changed attitudes or behaviours tend to be temporary and may be discarded once membership of that group is no longer important. This is not required in exams from 2012 onwards.

Evaluation of research into conformity

Limitations of Asch's research

Sampling limitations

Asch's original studies used only male students, drawn from three different colleges in the USA. This represents a limited sample in two respects:

- Type of participant – US students at the time were mostly White and middle class.
- Historical bias – McCarthyism exerted a strong influence to conform in the USA in the 1950s.

Asch's students admitted they felt they would have been ridiculed if they had not conformed, whereas in Perrin and Spencer's 1980 study, students admitted they felt they would have been ridiculed if they had conformed to the majority when they gave the wrong answer.

Methodological problems

One of the problems with Asch's experimental arrangement is that confederates (who were not trained actors) might have given the game away. Participants may simply have seen through the deception and therefore their choice might have reflected their interpretation of the reason for this deception rather than the need to conform.

Mori and Arai (2010) attempted to overcome this problem by using a technique where participants wore glasses with polarizing filters, so that different participants could view the same stimuli and yet see them differently. In this study, three participants wore identical glasses and one participant wore a different pair, which made a different comparison line appear to match the target line. Female participants' level of conformity matched the findings in Asch's original research, with just over one-third of the responses conforming to the view of the majority. However, male participants were not swayed by the majority decision, and conformity rates were very low compared to the original Asch study.

Lack of real-life validity

Mori and Arai (2010) argue that conformity generally takes place among people who are well acquainted, such as family members, friends or colleagues. They claim that in daily life we rarely have to make decisions among total strangers, as in Asch's study. In Mori and Arai's study, conformity was highest in the groups where the participants all knew each other. Conformity levels were lowest in the groups where the participants were strangers to each other.

An inappropriate emphasis on conformity

Although Asch's study produced a surprising level of conformity, we should remember that participants only conformed in one-third of the trials where the majority produced a unanimous wrong answer. In two-thirds of these 'critical' trials, the participants faced the same unanimous majority yet maintained their independence.

The Asch effect is an unstable phenomenon
Lalancette and Standing (1990) modified Asch's original study to make the test stimuli more ambiguous and so increase the likelihood of conformity. Despite this, however, they found no significant evidence of conformity among their participants, and so concluded that the so-called Asch effect was an unpredictable phenomenon rather than a stable aspect of human behaviour.

Other influences on conformity

Cultural differences
A **meta-analysis** of studies of conformity (Smith and Bond 1998) found that conformity levels were significantly higher in **collectivist** cultures (where interdependence is highly valued) than in individualist cultures (where independence is more highly valued). However, in cross-cultural comparisons, there is always the problem of relevance of the materials used; it is possible that the differences observed in these studies had more to do with differences in the meaningfulness of the task in these cultures than in differences in conformity.

Historical differences
Smith and Bond also established that there was a negative correlation between date of publication and levels of conformity found. Earlier studies, such as Asch, showed higher levels of conformity, whereas later studies, such as Perrin and Spencer, showed lower levels of conformity. However, Neto's (1995) more recent study in Portugal, using female students as participants, found that 59 per cent conformed on at least one of the 12 critical trials and 28 per cent conformed on between three and 12 trials.

Gender differences
Eagly and Carli (1981) carried out a meta-analysis of 145 studies and concluded that women were more likely to conform than men. They interpreted this as a consequence of differential socialization, whereby women are encouraged to be more dependent than men, and more motivated to seek approval through compliance.

However, they also found that male researchers were much more likely to find evidence of gender differences than were female researchers, and were more likely to use materials that were more familiar to males than females. When neutral materials were used, gender differences were less obvious.

Essential notes

Conformity is not a stable phenomenon across cultures and across time. Research across different types of cultures and across different points in historical time has resulted in significantly different levels of conformity.

Examiners' notes

If you choose to include cultural or gender differences as a way of evaluating Asch's conformity study, you should use these points in a suitably evaluative way – i.e. by using an AO2 'tag' such as 'However, research has shown that not every gender conforms to the same degree...' or by pointing out how gender and cultural differences contribute to a biased representation of conformity when only male US students are used in a particular study.

Explanations of conformity

Normative social influence

Human beings are a social species, which means they have a strong desire to be accepted and a fear of being rejected. This makes it difficult for individuals to deviate from the majority because it is important for them to be accepted within their reference group.

Normative social influence, therefore, is based on our desire to be liked by other members of the group. We conform because we believe that by doing this others will accept and approve of us. This type of influence produces a change in public behaviour (i.e. public compliance) where the individual goes along with the majority while privately still holding to their own views.

In interviews following the Asch study, most participants who had conformed to the majority even when the majority was wrong claimed they did it for this reason.

When are people most likely to conform to normative social influence?
According to Latané's **social impact theory**, we are most likely to conform to normative social influence when group membership is important to us. For example, in a study by Perrin and Spencer (1981), unemployed Black youths from a racially tense part of London were more likely to conform to a majority made up of other Black youths when the experimenter was White.

The effect of group size is less clear cut. Asch discovered that a majority of four would produce more conformity than a majority of three, but increasing the size of the majority above this figure did not produce significantly higher levels of conformity.

People are also more likely to conform when they perceive some cost associated with not conforming. Perrin and Spencer used students on probation, with a majority comprised of probation officers, and found a level of conformity only slightly less than that found by Asch in 1951.

Evaluation of normative social influence

The concept of normative social influence has been used to give an insight into why some children begin bullying other children, even though they are clearly uncomfortable with such behaviour. Garandeau and Cillessen (2006) found that children who had a greater need for social acceptance were the most likely to comply to pressure exerted by a bullying group to victimize another child. By conforming to the actions of the bullying group, these children believed they would be accepted by other group members, and so could maintain their friendship regardless of how they felt in private toward bullying.

Essential notes

Normative social influence is based on our desire to be liked by other members of the group. We conform so that others will accept and approve of us. This type of influence only produces public compliance.

Examiners' notes

The material on these two pages should prepare you for most types of question on why people conform, but you should be flexible in how you use this material. For example, a 3-mark question on normative social influence would require between 50 and 75 words drawn from either or both of the first two paragraphs. A 12-mark essay on both explanations would require equal amounts of AO1 and AO2, so about 300 or more words including material from the two evaluative paragraphs.

Informational social influence

Informational social influence is based on our desire to be right. It is based on **social comparison** – looking to others for guidance when we are not sure of the right way to behave, particularly in situations that are novel or ambiguous. In these situations, we look to others because we believe they have more 'information' about the situation than we do (even if they don't).

For example, informational social influence may be particularly strong when we move from one situation to another (e.g. from school to university) and so experience situational ambiguity. In these situations, individuals use others as a way of discovering the acceptable ways of behaving.

When are people most likely to conform to informational social influence?

Although situational ambiguity is the most important one, it is only one of the factors that might lead people to conform to informational social influence. In an emergency, we may not have time to think calmly; therefore, we look to others for information about the best course of action.

We are also more likely to conform if we believe the majority has more expertise or knowledge about the task. Allen (1980) suggested that intelligence was a major determining factor of conformity to informational social influence, with intelligent individuals being more self-confident and so less likely to conform.

Evaluation of informational social influence

Allen's suggestion that intelligence is a major determinant of conformity is challenged by Asch's original findings. Asch used students from three colleges, varying in terms of background, intelligence and so on. Although he found that highly intelligent students from a private college conformed less than students of moderate intelligence from a 'metropolitan' college, students considered to be of the lowest intelligence conformed mid-way between the two.

The informational social influence explanation is supported by research evidence. For example, Wittenbrink and Henly (1996) found that White participants who were exposed to negative information about African Americans that they thought was the view of the majority increased their prejudice scores. For example, they were more likely to overestimate the percentage of African Americans who had spent time in prison.

Essential notes

Informational social influence is based on our desire to be right and involves us in looking to others for the most appropriate ways to think or behave when we are unsure. It can result in private acceptance of the group's position as well as public compliance.

Examiners' notes

You may be asked to use the information on this spread to answer a question on a particular scenario – for instance to identify why a particular individual is conforming, and then answer further questions relating to this area, or possibly interpreting or commenting on some research methods questions linked to it.

Obedience to authority

Obedience is a form of social influence where an individual acts in response to a direct order from an authority figure. It is assumed that without this order, the person would not have acted in this way. Obedience may sometimes be destructive, such as when people comply with the orders of a malevolent authority. For example, the killings that took place as part of the My Lai massacre in Vietnam in 1968 were directly attributed to orders given by Lt William Calley.

Milgram's research into obedience

Essential notes

The impetus for Milgram's research came from claims during trials of war criminals such as Adolf Eichmann that they were 'only obeying orders'. It was Milgram's contention that insights from his studies were useful in understanding the psychological motivation for such crimes.

Milgram (1963) carried out a series of studies to find out whether ordinary Americans would obey an unjust order from a person in authority to inflict pain on another person. In particular, Milgram wanted to know what factors in a situation led people to obey.

Milgram's methodology

● Milgram's original study (referred to as the 'baseline study') used 40 male volunteers (not students) who were told that the study concerned the role of punishment in learning.

● The study took place in a laboratory at Yale University, and the experimenter wore a laboratory coat to reinforce his status and authority.

● Participants were deceived into thinking they were giving electric shocks to a 'learner' in a word-association task, but the shocks were not real and the learner was actually a confederate of the experimenter.

● In this study, the experimenter (the authority figure) was in the same room as the participant (the 'teacher'), and the learner was in a different room where he could not be seen or heard.

● The teacher was required to give increasing levels of shock as the learner began to make mistakes. The shocks went from an initial 15 volts to a maximum of 450 volts. Obedience was measured as the percentage of participants who went to this maximum shock level.

● If the teacher hesitated to deliver shocks or seemed reluctant to do so, the experimenter used a series of 'prods' to encourage them to continue.

Milgram's findings

● Forty psychiatrists at a leading medical school predicted that most participants would not go beyond 150 volts, yet 65 per cent of participants continued to administer the full 450 volts.

● Variations to the baseline study showed that the proximity of the learner decreased obedience. When the teacher and the learner were in the same room, obedience levels dropped to 40 per cent.

Examiners' notes

This material (on methodology) could be used to answer a question on 'How have psychologists investigated obedience?' However, if you are allocated just 6 marks for this, you need to précis the material in this section to about 120–150 words. Précis needs practice, but the added advantage when you précis material is you are also processing it, so making it more memorable. In questions on methodology, you should not include any material on findings.

- When the experimenter left the room and gave orders over the telephone, participants felt better able to defy authority and obedience levels dropped to 21 per cent.

- The most significant situational factor in determining the level of obedience was the action of confederates. When participants were paired with 'disobedient' confederates, who refused to continue shocking the learner, only 10 per cent continued to 450 volts. However, when participants were paired with an 'obedient' confederate, a massive 92.5 per cent continued to the full 450 volts.

Other research into obedience

Hofling *et al.* (1966)

Hofling and colleagues studied 22 nurses working on a night shift in a hospital. Each of the nurses received a phone call from an unknown doctor, who ordered them to administer 20 mg of a drug (given the made-up name 'Astroten') to a patient so that it would have taken effect before they arrived to treat them. Obeying this order would have broken several hospital rules, including giving twice the maximum dose allowable for this drug (clearly marked) and acting without a signed order from an unknown doctor.

Despite this, 21 of the 22 nurses started to give the medication (actually a harmless placebo) before being stopped by another nurse. When interviewed, the nurses claimed that 'this type of thing' had happened before, and because doctors became angry if they did not do as they were told, they felt compelled to obey. However, when a group of other nurses had the scenario described to them, almost all believed that the nurses would have refused to carry out the order in those circumstances.

Rank and Jacobson (1977)

Rank and Jacobson varied Hofling and colleagues' study. They were uneasy about the fact that the nurses in the Hofling study had no opportunity to seek advice from other nurses as, in most hospital situations, nurses would have had time to ask advice from nurses of equal or higher status. They replicated the procedure, but this time used a familiar drug – Valium – with the order coming from a familiar doctor, as well as allowing nurses the time to speak to other nurses before carrying out the order. With these changes, the researchers found that only two out of 18 nurses went to the point of being about to administer the drug as they were ordered.

Evaluation of research into obedience

Validity

Internal validity is a measure of whether the experimental procedures used in a study actually work and whether the effects observed are genuine. In the Milgram study, this would include whether participants believed they were really delivering electric shocks. **External validity** refers to the degree to which the findings of a study can be generalized to other situations outside the laboratory (e.g. whether Milgram's study tells us anything about obedience in real life).

Internal validity

Orne and Holland (1968) claimed that participants in Milgram's study were merely 'going along' with their role as research participants and did not truly believe they were delivering real electric shocks. They claimed that participants' stress was not real either, but was part of the pretence of the role, with the main motivation being to please the experimenter.

Milgram disputed both these claims. He cited evidence from recordings of the study which clearly showed real distress in the participants. He also referred to evidence from post-experimental interviews, where over 80 per cent of participants admitted to believing that they were giving real shocks.

Sheridan and King (1972) overcame the uncertainty over whether participants did or did not believe they were giving electric shocks by having participants give real electric shocks to a puppy every time it failed to solve a discrimination test. The percentage of students who went to the maximum shock level (although only a mild shock was actually delivered) was roughly the same as that found in Milgram's study.

External validity

Milgram's findings have been reproduced in a number of other settings and cultures. For example, Mantell (1971) found higher levels of obedience in a German sample, although lower rates of obedience were found in an Australian study (Kilham and Mann 1971). Kilham and Mann found 40 per cent obedience rates for males and 16 per cent for females.

The real test of external validity, however, is whether these findings can be generalized to real-life settings. Orne and Holland claimed that the situation in Milgram's laboratory bore little resemblance to real-life situations where obedience was required. For example, Mandel (1998) argued that Milgram's conclusions about the relevance of obedience to situations such as the Holocaust are unjustified and are not borne out by an examination of real-life events.

He quotes the study of Reserve Police Battalion 101 (Browning 1992) to support this claim. For these men, required to carry out executions of Jews during the Holocaust, situational factors such as physical proximity to their victims and an absent authority figure made no difference to whether they 'obeyed' or not.

Mandel concludes that the 'only obeying orders' explanation for these events constitutes an **obedience alibi**. He argues that the zeal with which many of the men of Reserve Police Battalion 101 killed their victims pointed to a deep-seated hatred of the Jews rather than a group of men reluctantly 'obeying orders'.

Ethics

Milgram's study of obedience has attracted a good deal of ethical criticism from other psychologists (such as Diana Baumrind 1964).

- Lack of respect for participants – Baumrind claimed that Milgram showed insufficient respect for his participants and took insufficient steps to protect them from psychological harm. Baumrind believed that participants were under great emotional strain during the study, which had the potential to cause them long-term harm. She believed this could not be justified given the aims of the study. Despite this claim, the **APA** investigated Milgram's study after its publication and found it ethically acceptable.

- Deception and lack of consent – For the experiment to work, deception was essential. For example, participants were told the study was interested in the relationship between punishment and learning rather than the true purpose of the study. Without knowing the real purpose of the study, participants could not give their informed consent to participation.

- Impact on ethical guidelines – A positive outcome of Milgram's study has been the increased awareness among psychologists concerning how they should treat their participants. This has led to developments in ethical guidelines that place the welfare of the participant above the interests of the researcher. Because of the controversy created by Milgram's research, the APA developed its own ethical guidelines, which were formalized in 1973.

Replications of Milgram's research

Burger (2007) carried out a partial replication of Milgram's study taking care to address all of the problematic ethical issues in the original study. Burger only took his participants to 150 volts (80 per cent of those who reached this level in Milgram's original study then went on to 450 volts). However, unlike Milgram, Burger went out of his way to protect the welfare of his participants. For example, all participants were carefully screened and monitored throughout the study, and their right to withdraw was constantly emphasized. Despite these differences from the original study, 70 per cent of participants ignored the victim's pleas and obeyed the authority figure.

Examiners' notes

Some students present a 'list' of evaluative points in their answers, but fail to flesh any of these out. A common failing is to describe Milgram's study as 'shocking' or to say that he deceived his participants, without adding any extra detail. You will always get higher marks if you elaborate your criticisms, so don't try to include too many points in your evaluation and practise fleshing out the ones that you do choose.

Essential notes

Replications of Milgram's research are generally not allowed under **BPS** or APA guidelines. Burger only managed to get ethical approval for his study by addressing all the ethical issues that had been criticized in the original Milgram study.

Explanations of why people obey

Gradual commitment

Milgram found that once participants had committed themselves to giving low levels of shock, they found it harder to resist the demands of the experimenter to give gradually increasing levels of shock because each voltage increment was fairly small. For example, in Milgram's study, 80 per cent of those who administered 150 volts went on to deliver the maximum 450-volt shock.

Psychologists refer to this gradual commitment as the foot-in-the-door effect. Once people comply with a fairly trivial, relatively harmless request, in order to appear consistent they find it more difficult to refuse to carry out more serious, escalating requests.

Commentary on gradual commitment

Lifton (1986) provided support for the gradual commitment explanation in his study of Nazi doctors working at Auschwitz. These doctors were first required to carry out sterilizations (e.g. of mental defectives), but having committed to that order, were then required to carry out more and more horrific medical experiments, ending with the killing of their 'subjects' in the interests of science.

In the context of mass violence, this is commonly called 'the slippery slope'. For example, the Nazis did not begin with death camps, but started with laws that discriminated against Jews in less extreme ways, such as removing rights and property. Each successive step escalated the previous one, until eventually the death camps were established and accepted by those who operated them.

The role of buffers

'Buffer' describes anything that protects the individual from having to confront the consequences of their actions. In Milgram's baseline study, the teacher and learner were in different rooms, so the teacher was 'buffered' from seeing the 'victim' in distress. Milgram believed that buffers acted as a mechanism to help people reduce the strain of having to obey an unjust or immoral command.

Commentary on the role of buffers

Support for the influence of buffers in obedience is evident in situations of mass violence. For example, in the early years of the Holocaust, Jews were killed by mobile killing squads, such as Reserve Police Battalion 101. However, the physical proximity to their victims had a disturbing psychological effect on the killers, so gas chambers were designed to separate the killers physically from their victims.

Agentic shift

Milgram believed that people usually operate in an autonomous state, behaving voluntarily and aware of the consequences of their actions.

In some circumstances, however, they may enter an agentic state, seeing themselves acting as the agent of another person and hence not responsible for their actions.

The movement from autonomous to agentic state is known as **agentic shift**. In the agentic state, argued Milgram, participants would mindlessly accept the orders of the authority figure, claiming that they were only doing what they were told. Many Nazi war criminals claimed that they were not responsible for their actions, but 'only obeying orders'.

Commentary on agentic shift

Milgram believed the concept of agentic shift explained the behaviour of his obedient participants and events during the Holocaust. However, Mandel (1998) argued that this comparison was inappropriate. For example, Milgram's participants were involved for just half an hour, whereas Holocaust perpetrators carried out their duties over several years. Milgram's agentic shift explanation also fails to explain the type of gradual and irreversible conversion process that Lifton (1986) observed in Nazi doctors at Auschwitz. Lifton claims that situations requiring recurrent acts of evil over a considerable length of time change the way the individual thinks and behaves even when they are not acting under the orders of authority.

Personality factors

It is possible that some people have personality characteristics that predispose them to obedience (i.e. they are more prone to obedience), such as:

- Authoritarian personality – Milgram found that participants who were highly authoritarian tended to display higher levels of obedience than those who were less authoritarian. People with an authoritarian personality tend to be hostile towards minorities but submissive to those in authority.
- Psychopathic personality – Miale and Selzer (1975) claimed that the obedience shown by some of Milgram's participants was a socially acceptable way of expressing their psychopathic impulses.

Commentary on personality factors

Milgram rejected the claim that those participants who were most obedient possessed either an authoritarian personality or psychopathic tendencies, which are both relatively uncommon. He pointed out that his sample comprised ordinary people who had volunteered, and their behaviour could better be explained by the concept of agentic shift.

Arendt (1963) challenged the claim that destructive obedience was the expression of psychopathic impulses. She covered the trial of Adolf Eichmann, who orchestrated the mass murder of Jews during the Holocaust, yet claimed at his trial that he had 'only been obeying orders'. Arendt claimed that Eichmann seemed perfectly normal, showing no signs of psychopathic tendencies.

Essential notes

Milgram emphasized the importance of situational factors in obedience and therefore rejected the role played by dispositional factors (such as personality) in determining obedience. This does not, however, mean that they have no part in determining the likelihood of a person obeying authority.

Independent behaviour: resisting pressures to conform and obey

Resisting conformity

Research on conformity has discovered the conditions that are most likely to lead to conformity, but has also highlighted when people might resist pressures to conform.

Desire for individuation

The desire to maintain a sense of individuality sometimes outweighs pressure to conform. Asch discovered that many of the participants who responded to majority influence with independence were less concerned with social norms than those who conformed.

Snyder and Fromkin (1980) established that both extreme similarity and extreme uniqueness are unpleasant states and lead to behavioural attempts to re-establish the opposite state. In their research, participants who were told their most important attitudes were nearly identical to most other people subsequently resisted pressures to conform more than those who were told their attitudes were different from most people.

Prior commitment

Once people publicly commit themselves to a position, they are less likely to change their opinions than if they hold this position only in private. In Deutsch and Gerard's 1955 variation of Asch's procedure, the naïve participant gave their judgement before the majority gave a unanimous, different answer. When offered the chance to reconsider, the participant almost never did, fearing to appear indecisive. This demonstrated the importance of prior commitment in resisting subsequent pressures to conform.

The role of allies

Asch discovered that the introduction of a confederate who also went against the majority caused conformity levels to drop below 10 per cent. Having an ally appeared to build confidence and aid resistance because the participant was no longer facing a unanimous majority. The fellow dissenter provides the naïve participant with an assessment of reality, making them more confident in their ability to reject the majority decision.

Asch found that conformity levels dropped even when the dissenter gave a different wrong answer, which suggests that it is breaking the group's consensus that is important in resisting pressures to conform.

Time to think

Zimbardo (2007) advises that people should be mindful of how situational factors can pressurize us to conform, and we should engage critical thinking, avoiding mindless conformity to the majority. Asking whether the action conflicts with our moral code helps us consider whether we want to compromise our opinion of ourselves to gain others' approval. Zimbardo

Examiners' notes

Make sure you are fully aware of the difference between conformity, obedience and minority influence, and that you use insights from the appropriate area of research to answer questions. Conformity research is restricted to *majority* influence, therefore material related to *minority* influence is not relevant and would not be creditworthy.

Essential notes

These ideas are expanded in Zimbardo's book *The Lucifer Effect*. You can also read more about this by visiting the dedicated website at www.lucifereffect.com.

also suggests taking a future perspective and imagining what we might later think of our current conforming action.

Resisting obedience

A significant number of participants in Milgram's study refused to obey beyond a certain shock level. Milgram identified those factors that contributed to a person's ability to resist pressures to obey a malevolent authority figure.

Questioning the motives and status of authority

Questioning the motives, legitimacy and expertise of authority figures might increase resistance to automatic obedience. When Milgram's study was moved from the prestigious surroundings of Yale University to some run-down offices in the commercial quarter, participants found it easier to question the legitimacy of the experimenter's instructions. As a result, more participants felt able to resist the experimenter, and obedience levels dropped to 48 per cent (from 65 per cent). This suggests that the status of the authority figure and the setting is a key factor in obedience and its resistance.

Disobedient models

Resistance was also increased in the presence of disobedient models (i.e. seeing others refuse to obey instructions from an authority figure). For example, in one variation of Milgram's study, two confederates assisted the naïve participant in their role of 'teacher'. However, when the two confederates refused to continue beyond the 210-volt level, 90 per cent of the naïve participants also rebelled and refused to continue.

The presence of disobedient models undermines the experimenter's authority and makes it more likely that the individual will have the confidence to resist subsequent pressures to obey. This was demonstrated in real life during the Rosenstrasse protest in 1943 (see p.43), where women felt better able to resist orders to disband because of the presence of other, disobedient, role models who also demanded the release of their Jewish husbands.

Feeling responsible and empathetic

In Milgram's study, some participants disobeyed the experimenter when they believed the learner was in distress. For these individuals, even imagining the suffering of the person receiving the electric shocks was sufficient to lead to an **empathetic** response and a refusal to continue. Other teachers were protected from imagining the learner's suffering when the learner was in a separate room, but when this buffer was removed and they were in the same room, the teacher felt more personally responsible for their suffering. Visual cues associated with the victim's suffering are believed to trigger empathetic responses, giving the 'teacher' a more complete understanding of the victim's experience, making them more likely to resist pressure to obey.

Examiners' notes

You should be able to work out the situational conditions that made it easier for participants to resist the authority figure by examining the changes in obedience levels in the different variations, e.g. when the authority figure was absent, when there were disobedient confederates and so on. This information can be used to elaborate your explanations.

Examiners' notes

Many students tell the story of one female participant who had lived through the Holocaust and seen the horrors of mindless obedience. This insight is appropriate, but should not be used without a full contextual explanation (i.e. bringing out the conditions of empathy for the 'learner').

External locus of control

What happens is outside your control
(e.g. caused by fate)

Internal locus of control

What happens to you is within your
control (e.g. your hard work)

Fig. 3
Locus of control

Independent behaviour: locus of control

Rotter's **locus of control (LOC)** refers to individual differences in people's beliefs and expectation about what controls events in their lives. There are two extremes, as shown in Fig. 3, although most people fall somewhere between these two extremes.

Internality and externality

● People with an internal LOC believe that what happens to them is largely a consequence of their own ability or effort – they can therefore control events in their life. People high in internality tend to display independence in thoughts and behaviour, and as active seekers of information rely less on the opinions of others. This means they are better able to resist social influence.

● People with an external LOC tend to believe that what happens to them is controlled by external factors, such as the actions of others or luck. They have a sense that things 'just happen to them' and are largely uncontrollable. They tend to approach events with a more passive and fatalistic attitude, taking less personal responsibility for their actions.

Research on locus of control

Holland (1967)
Holland carried out a number of experimental variations of Milgram's procedures, comparing obedience levels for internals and externals, as measured on Rotter's Internal/External Locus of Control Scale. He found no significant relationship between locus of control scores and obedience levels. However, Blass (1991) carried out a replication of Holland's study and discovered that participants with an internal locus of control were more resistant to pressures to obey, particularly when they felt they were being coerced and manipulated by the experimenter.

Schurz (1985)
In an Austrian study, participants were instructed to apply increasing levels of ultrasound stimulation, which they were told could cause skin damage at the highest level of a 20-step continuum. Schurz found that 80 per cent of participants pressed all 20 switches as instructed by the experimenter, but locus of control scores were not predictive of obedience. However, participants who maintained their independence and refused to continue to the final level had a greater tendency to accept responsibility for their actions (a characteristic of internal individuals) than did obedient participants.

Twenge *et al.* (2004)
Twenge and colleagues carried out a meta-analysis of studies of young Americans and found that their locus of control scores had become increasingly more external between 1960 and 2002. Participants tended to believe that their fate (and that of the world in general) was determined

by luck and powerful others rather than their own actions. Twenge and colleagues attributed this trend to social factors such as unemployment, increasing divorce rates and other factors that led young people to believe that many aspects of their lives were beyond their control.

There are both positive and negative consequences of this trend towards increasing externality:

- The upside is that younger generations would display less prejudice and a greater tolerance toward individuals regardless of their background (believing that situational factors shape everybody's life).
- The negative consequence is that high levels of externality are associated with poor school achievement and depression.

Not all research has shown this trend towards increasing externality. For example, a Chinese study (Tong and Wang 2006) showed that Chinese employees today reported relatively more internal locus of control than in previous years.

Gender and cultural differences in locus of control

Gender differences

Research has found that there are gender differences in locus of control, with males typically being found to be more internal than females (e.g. De Man *et al.* 1985). However, Schultz and Schultz (2005) found no significant differences in locus of control for adults in a US population. However, they did note that there may be specific sex-based differences for specific aspects of locus of control (e.g. they cite evidence that men may have a greater internal locus for questions related to academic achievement). A study by McGinnies *et al.* (1974) found that females across five different cultures were significantly more external than males, a difference attributed to the perceived opportunities available to the different sexes in those cultures.

Cultural differences

Research has shown that people from different cultures may also vary in terms of their locus of control. For example, McGinnies and colleagues found that Japanese people are more external than people in Australia and the USA. Berry *et al.* (1992), on the other hand, found that the differences in locus of control scores between different countries in Europe tended to be small. Cultural differences, such as those found between Japanese and American individuals, suggest that locus of control may be passed on as part of a culture's tradition.

Differences in locus of control may also be found within the same culture. For example, Dyal (1984) found that ethnic groups differ in terms of their locus of control. In a US sample, Black people were significantly more external than White people.

Minority influence

Social influence is not only the product of majority influence, as history is littered with examples of social changes that have begun with the influence of a deviant minority.

How does minority influence work?

Creating attention

Deviant minorities draw attention to the issues that may otherwise have been ignored by the majority. If a person is exposed to an argument that contradicts the current view of the majority, this creates a conflict, which the individual is motivated to reduce. They may achieve this by examining the views of the minority more closely to better understand why they don't hold the same view as the majority. Nemeth (2003) argues that the power of minorities is, therefore, that they stimulate thought so that over time people may be converted to a new way of thinking and behaving.

Consistency

Consistency is generally recognized as the single most important factor for a minority to be influential. Initially, members of the majority may simply dismiss the minority point of view, but if the minority are consistent, the majority may take their position more seriously. There are two types of consistency:

- Intra-individual consistency – where individual members of the minority maintain a consistent position over time
- Inter-individual consistency – where there is agreement among the different members of the minority.

Augmentation

The augmentation principle states that the minority position may be re-evaluated by the majority if it still occurs despite difficult circumstances. Minorities frequently suffer for their views at the hands of the majority. However, according to the augmentation principle, their impact is increased (i.e. augmented) because the minority is seen to be willing to make sacrifices to get their point across.

The snowball effect

The term '**snowball effect**' is used to describe the mass movement of members of the majority toward the minority position. Once a few members of the majority start to move toward the minority position, the influence of the minority begins to gather momentum as more and more people convert to the minority position. As more people defect to this position, it 'punches a hole' in the illusion of majority unanimity and decreases the pressure to conform to the majority position.

The dissociation model

Perez *et al.* (1995) propose that minority groups tend to influence the majority over a much longer time frame compared with majority influence.

Essential notes

Minority influence is a form of social influence where majority group members reject the established group norm and gradually move toward the position being championed by the minority.

Essential notes

Failure to show both types of consistency may undermine the credibility of the minority in the eyes of the majority. If the minority remains consistent, however, the majority assumes that they must really believe in the position they are putting forward.

This is because the minority group position is frequently rejected because majority group members do not want to associate themselves with a deviant minority.

Over time, however, minority ideas may be assimilated into the majority viewpoint without those in the majority remembering where those ideas first came from. In such circumstances, the content and the original source of the content become dissociated. When messages become dissociated from their source, majority group members are able to avoid identification with a deviant minority, while still being influenced by their ideas.

An example of social change through minority influence

The suffragettes were able to produce social change by using the techniques of minority influence. By holding constant rallies and producing educational pamphlets, they were able to create a conflict in the minds of majority group members, drawing their attention to the idea of votes for women.

The suffragettes maintained their position over 15 years and were consistent in their arguments regardless of the attitudes of those around them. Their fight for the vote continued even when faced with imprisonment or death by hunger strike. As a result, majority group members were more likely to take their views seriously and be affected by them because of the augmentation principle. Acceptance of the suffragette position was gradual, suggesting a 'snowball effect' in political opinion.

Evaluation of minority influence

Minorities may stimulate the majority to consider social change
Because minorities advocate a new way of thinking, their views, even when they are wrong, stimulate the kinds of thought processes that raise the quality of decision-making within the majority. As a result, minorities stimulate majority group members to expend more cognitive effort and to think in more creative ways about an issue, and so increase the likelihood of social change.

Minorities may not lead to greater processing of their message
Mackie (1987) claims the views of the minority do not lead to more careful processing of their message. We tend to believe that the majority of group members share similar beliefs to our own (the **false consensus effect**). If the majority expresses a viewpoint different to ours, we are motivated to consider it carefully to understand why it is different. In contrast, claims Mackie, people tend not to waste time processing why a minority's viewpoint is different, resulting in the minority being less influential in the process of social change.

Examiners' notes
The topic of social change requires you to understand the underlying psychological principles that influence people's behaviour (e.g. the need to conform, factors that facilitate resistance to obedience and so on) and also the ability to illustrate these principles in real-life examples of social change.

Essential notes
The campaigning Women's Social and Political Union was founded in 1903 by Emmeline Pankhurst and her daughters Christabel and Sylvia. Women were finally given the vote in 1918, when women over 30 were allowed to vote, and in 1928 this was extended to all women over the age of 21.

Examiners' notes
The information on pp. 40–3 should provide you with information to answer most questions on social change (e.g. a 6-mark description of the relationship between minority influence and social change, or a more general 6-mark description about social influence research and social change). You might be asked to apply this understanding to a novel situation involving social change or (perhaps the most demanding) to construct a 12-mark essay that contains equal amounts of AO1 and AO2. The secret to success, as always, is to prepare for all these types of questions and *practise* answering them.

Understanding social change

The term '**social change**' refers to a major change in the social structure of a society, or some widespread change in the behaviour of the individuals that make up that society. Social change may refer to social progress or social revolution, such as the Communist Revolution in the former Soviet Union, or to social movements, such as the suffragettes or the Civil Rights movement in the USA.

Social change through majority influence

The power of normative social influence has been used to bring about social change (e.g. in energy conservation initiatives). People have a strong desire to be accepted by members of their peer group. This makes it difficult for them to deviate from what they believe to be the majority position because they use the group norm as a reference for their own behaviour.

Conserving energy

Nolan *et al.* (2007) placed door hangers on the doors of San Diego residents once a week for a month. The door hangers carried one of four messages, one of which stated that the majority of their neighbours regularly tried to conserve energy (information that had been learned from a prior survey). The researchers also included a control group of residents whose door hanger simply encouraged energy conservation but provided no rationale for this. Only information regarding their neighbours' energy usage led to significant decreases in residents' energy consumption.

Saving the environment

Goldstein *et al.* (2007) followed this with a study attempting to change hotel guest behaviour by encouraging them to reuse their towels. They compared the impact of four types of door hanger, including 'Help save the environment' and 'Help save resources for future generations', followed by information stressing respect for nature. A final type of card stated 'Join your fellow citizens in helping to save the environment', followed by information that the majority of hotel guests did reuse their towels when asked. Compared to the other messages, the final 'group norm' message increased towel reuse by an average of 34 per cent.

Social change through minority influence

Minorities tend to be in a disadvantaged position, either numerically or in terms of their lack of social power. Therefore, they are unlikely to have the power to influence other people on a wide scale. In addition, by challenging the status quo, they are threatening the social order. This increases the likelihood that they will be perceived as deviant by the majority. Consequently, all minorities face the double challenge of avoiding being portrayed as deviants, and of making others embrace their position. Despite this, minorities frequently strive for direct influence as they attempt to bring about social change by means of consistency and the augmentation principle.

Examiners' notes

The previous section on minority influence may also be used to answer a general question on social change, or a specific one on 'minority influence and social change.' The material on these pages offers more general material relating to the relationship between social influence research and social change.

Essential notes

Terrorism refers to 'the use or threat of serious violence to advance some kind of cause'. Kruglanski believes that the aim of terrorism is to bring about social change when direct social force is not possible.

Terrorism and minority influence

Kruglanski (2003) argues that many acts of terrorism are intended to bring about social change through minority influence. This view that terrorism may use the methods of minority influence is supported by the following observations:

- *Consistency* – The influence of a minority is most effective when it is consistent. Kruglanski claims that the frequent suicide bombings in Afghanistan and Iraq are an example of consistency of expression of the minority position.
- *Augmentation* – Because many members of the minority may die 'for their cause', this may bring about social change by conveying the desperation of the minority group and their willingness to suffer for their beliefs. This is likely to result in members of the majority group taking the minority position seriously.

Obedience research and social change

Aspects of Milgram's work have provided an insight into how social change might be achieved, particularly in the role of peers in resisting a malevolent authority. In Milgram's 'two peers rebel' study, three 'teachers' shared the task of delivering shocks when the learner made mistakes. Two of the teachers (who were actually confederates of the experimenter) refused to continue beyond 210 volts. The naïve participant was then instructed to take over shocking the learner alone. The overwhelming majority of participants took the opportunity to defy the experimenter and refused to deliver any more shocks.

Civil disobedience: The Rosenstrasse protest

There is historical evidence to support the power of disobedient peers to help bring about social change. In 1943, Nazi troops began the roundup of intermarried Jews, detaining them in the Rosentrasse in Berlin prior to moving them to concentration camps. A crowd of 200 women (German women married to Jewish men) gathered and began chanting 'We want our husbands back'. The women were ordered to disperse, but refused, and the chanting continued. At one point, troops set up machine guns in front of the building and threatened to fire into the crowd of women.

Eventually, the women's resistance was rewarded, with the release of the intermarried Jews. The psychological isolation of each individual dissenter at the Rosenstrasse, as with the individual participants in Milgram's study, meant that resistance was risky, but the presence of others who were also willing to resist gave each individual woman the confidence to stand up to a powerful authority.

The implications of this protest are that if such protests had spread across Germany, they might have prevented the genocide that resulted in the deaths of over six million Jews between 1938 and 1945.

Examiners' notes

You can use the historical examples given here as AO2 evaluation to offer evidence to support the claims that social influence research can inform us about social change. However, if a question is AO1 only (e.g. 'Outline how social influence research helps us to understand social change'), you can use this material to extend your description of the relationship between social influence and social change.

Definitions of abnormality

The term 'abnormal' literally means 'not normal or usual', but beneath this simple statement lies a very complex area of psychology. One major difficulty centres on defining precisely what is meant by the term 'abnormality', as there is no single characteristic that applies to all instances of abnormal behaviour. Furthermore, defining psychological abnormality also has ethical, practical and personal consequences for individuals labelled 'abnormal'.

Deviation from social norms

Social norms are the rules that a society has about how people should think and behave. These rules may be:

- *explicit* – i.e. set down as codes of conduct or laws; breaking these rules (e.g. by dropping litter, violently attacking someone or stealing a car) may result in punishment
- *implicit* – i.e. 'understood' but not stated formally; for example, we have implicit rules about respecting personal space and how to behave in social situations (e.g. queuing in bars or at checkouts).

Abnormal behaviour can, therefore, be regarded as anything that deviates significantly from a social norm. For example, hugging and kissing a total stranger as if they are your best friend would be generally regarded as a violation of social norms. The question is, though, whether this deviant behaviour is an indication of a mental health problem or is just slightly odd or eccentric (by someone with an outgoing nature). In fact, this behaviour *is* commonly exhibited by people with **reactive attachment disorder** and may be one of the 'symptoms' used by professionals to diagnose that condition.

Failure to function adequately (FFA)

The basis of this definition of abnormality is that we can assess a person's mental state by judging how well they are functioning in aspects of everyday living – in other words, how well they are coping with life. Using the FFA definition, people may be defined as abnormal if they show themselves unable to deal with demands such as taking care of personal hygiene, eating properly or at all, holding down a job, interacting meaningfully with other people and so on. Rosenhan and Seligman (1989) identified seven characteristics that define a person's failure to function adequately:

- suffering or showing distress
- maladaptiveness (being unable adapt to situations, e.g. find fulfilling relationships or satisfying work)
- vividness and unconventionality (standing out)
- unpredictability and loss of control
- irrationality/incomprehensibility (behaviour that makes no sense to others)
- causing observer discomfort
- violating moral/social standards.

Essential notes

On pp. 44–5 we consider three definitions of abnormality and, on pp. 46–7, possible limitations with them.

Essential notes

Social norms are set by social groups and may, therefore, vary from culture to culture. For example, keeping a certain distance from someone you are talking to may be regarded as normal and polite in one culture, but standoffish in another culture. This is one of the limitations of this definition of abnormality and is examined further on pp. 46–7.

Examiners' notes

Questions can be asked that require you to apply your knowledge of the different definitions of abnormality to a novel situation. For example, you may be given some characteristics of a person's actions and have to match these with one of the definitions of abnormality covered on these two pages.

Sue *et al.* (1994) distilled this into the following three most common indications of a failure to function:

- *discomfort* – unusually intense, prolonged or exaggerated psychological (e.g. anxiety) and/or physiological symptoms (e.g. fatigue), or behaviour which causes onlookers to feel uncomfortable
- *bizarreness* – vivid and unusual experiences or behaviour, such as hallucinations, delusions, or inappropriate exposure
- *inefficiency* – barely functioning in everyday activities and occupations and/or failure to achieve potential, e.g. not eating, not attending school.

Professionals may use formal criteria for assessing a person's ability (or failure) to function, such as the Global Assessment of Functioning Scale (GAF) (see 'Essential notes').

Deviation from ideal mental health

A very different approach to identifying abnormality is Marie Jahoda's deviation from ideal mental health definition. Rather than focusing on the (negative) signs of illness, she proposed looking at the elements that make up a positive state of 'mental health'. Using this definition, abnormality can be seen as any significant deviation from this ideal (Jahoda 1958).

Jahoda identified six criteria that, if lacking in a person, might make them vulnerable to mental illness:

1. *Positive attitudes towards the self* – Having a positive self-concept and a sense of identity, encompassing qualities such as self-respect, self-confidence, self-reliance and self-acceptance. Without this, people may develop a negative self-concept or low self-esteem (perhaps because of the way others treat them).
2. *Self-actualization of one's potential* – Maslow (1968) suggested that we all have potential (e.g. intellectual, artistic, athletic) and we constantly strive to fulfil this potential. Mental health problems may occur if we are prevented from fulfilling it.
3. *Resistance to stress* – The ability to tolerate anxiety without falling to pieces, using effective coping strategies for dealing with stressful situations. Those less resistant to stress and anxiety may be more likely to develop psychological problems.
4. *Personal autonomy* – Relying on one's own inner resources and staying stable even in the face of setbacks and frustrations.
5. *Accurate perception of reality* – Viewing oneself and the world in realistic terms, rather than in a distorted way (whether that is a deluded view of one's good qualities or a pessimistic view of oneself as worthless).
6. *Adapting to and mastering the environment* – Being competent in all areas of life (at work, in personal relationships and in leisure activities) and being able to adapt and adjust to change. Someone fixed in old ways of thinking may appear abnormal to younger people and to those who have adapted to a changing environment.

This topic continues on the next spread. ☛

Essential notes

The Global Assessment of Functioning Scale (GAF) is part of the widely use **Diagnostic and Statistical Manual of Mental Disorders (DSM)**. It consists of psychological, social and occupational criteria that enable doctors to assess a person's ability to function normally and place them on a scale.

Aspects of functioning identified on the GAF include:

- *psychological* – ranging from difficulty in concentrating, through occasional panic attacks to delusions and hallucinations, and suicide attempts
- *social* – ranging from finding it hard to make or keep friends, to wholly inappropriate communications and grossly inappropriate behaviour in social situations
- *occupational* – ranging from difficulties in holding down a job to failure to maintain personal hygiene.

Essential notes

Humanistic psychologists such as Rogers (1902–87) suggest that mentally healthy people can engage in personal growth and eventual self-actualization. Abnormality, therefore, includes failure to function positively as well as failure to grow psychologically.

Evaluation of the approaches to defining abnormality

Although the three approaches outlined on pp. 44–5 are different, they share several strengths and weaknesses. Additional limitations of each definition are also given, opposite.

A gateway to treatment

All three approaches can help lay people to decide whether to seek professional help if they or others are concerned about deviant behaviour, failure to function or deviation from ideal mental health. Intuitive judgements can be made to help decide whether the behaviour in question is doing harm or is simply a one-off or merely eccentric.

Relating definitions to changing contexts and times

Some social norms are enshrined in law, whereas others are much more loosely defined, making it difficult to decide where the boundary between normal and abnormal lies. This is further complicated by:

- *Context* – The same behaviour can be judged as a violation of social norms or not in different contexts; for example, nudity in a sauna is more acceptable than nudity in a shopping mall.
- *Time* – Social norms change with the times; for example, homosexual acts were criminal offences in the UK until 1967. Twenty years later, the BBC broadcast the first gay kiss on British television in the soap opera *Eastenders*.

If there is ambiguity about the context or whether the time is right, people may unknowingly fall foul of 'the rules' and have their behaviour labelled abnormal.

Definitions of 'failure to function adequately' and 'ideal mental health' are also affected by time and place. For example:

- Binge drinking could be seen as normal on a night out, but not first thing in the morning when it would clearly render the person unable to function effectively.
- Keeping a 'stiff upper lip' (i.e. suppressing emotions) might be seen as an ideal mental state during wartime but as failing to face your problems in peacetime.

Cultural limitations

All three ways of defining abnormality are open to **cultural bias**. Cultural norms, standards or ideals are set by the dominant social group, lack objectivity, and change with time and place. If they are applied indiscriminately they could lead to under- or overdiagnosis; for example:

- Women are more frequently diagnosed than men with anxiety and depression (Sampson 1993).
- African-Caribbean immigrants are more frequently diagnosed than Caucasians with schizophrenia (Cochrane 1977).

These differences in frequency might be real, but we should also be open to the possibility that they are affected by cultural bias.

Examiners' notes

It is important to remember the context of the evaluation. The important point here is that definitions of abnormality are affected by time and place – *not* that people may binge drink or 'keep a stiff upper lip'.

Essential notes

Some conditions are peculiar to particular cultures and defy classification by Western diagnostic system. These are called culture-bound syndromes. An example is the South-East Asian condition *koro*, which is a fear of fatal retraction of the genitals into the abdomen.

Limitations of the deviation from social norms definition

- *Eccentric or abnormal?* – People regularly deviate from social norms without it being suggested they have a psychological abnormality. For example, someone who dresses only in black and wears black make-up may be regarded as 'odd' rather than abnormal in a pathological sense. However, if someone claims to chat regularly with the Angel Gabriel, then we might suspect a mental disorder. Thus, only particular kinds of 'abnormal' behaviour tend to be regarded as pathological.

- *Abnormal or criminal?* – People who violate legal norms are usually regarded as showing criminal behaviour, yet behaviour such as stealing cars is rarely attributed to underlying psychological disorder. With other crimes, such as mass murder or child abuse, there is a tendency to regard the perpetrators as abnormal and having an inbuilt fault in their personality, because 'normal' people couldn't commit such crimes. However, studies in social psychology have shown that, in certain circumstances, so-called 'normal' people can behave in shocking and antisocial ways (e.g. football hooligans).

Limitations of the FFA definition

- *Not the whole picture* – Failing to function adequately is not a true definition of 'abnormality'. Rather, it is a way of determining the extent of a person's problems and the likelihood that they might need professional help. Comer (2005) points out that psychological abnormality is not necessarily indicated by dysfunction alone. For example, being 'unpredictable' and 'out of control' (see Rosenhan and Seligman's criteria on p. 44) may simply be a sign that someone is drunk.

- *Exceptions to the rule* – A person who has just lost a loved one may show signs of 'maladaptiveness' or 'suffering', but few people would regard this as abnormal behaviour. Conversely, sociopaths (people with antisocial personalities) might exhibit violent or aggressive behaviour but show no sign of distress or dysfunction because they have no moral compass.

Limitations of the ideal mental health definition

- *The difficulty of self-actualizing* – Meeting all six of Jahoda's criteria appears quite demanding, and very few people may actually achieve their full potential in life, whether because of personal failings or a difficult environment. If self-actualization is a criterion for ideal mental health, then most of us would be regarded as mentally unhealthy.

- *Possible benefits of stress* – Some people actually work more efficiently in stressful situations. For example, some actors say that, despite feeling crippled by stress, it is an essential part of their working life and spurs them to give of their best.

- *A Western approach* – Jahoda's ideas are based on Western ideals of individuality. In **collectivist cultures**, importance is placed on promoting family ties and being part of a community; striving for individual self-fulfilment could then be regarded as abnormal.

Essential notes

The definition of 'deviant' behaviour appears to depend on a person crossing a particular line (in terms of severity or magnitude of behaviour), but it is often far from clear where the line lies.

Biological approach to psychopathology

Assumptions of the biological approach

The biological or biomedical approach to abnormality views psychological disorders as having biological or biochemical causes. Psychological disorders are seen as mental illnesses that, like physical illnesses, can be classified and treated by medical means. Psychopathology is thought to result from one of four main causes: infection, genetic factors, biochemistry or brain damage.

Infection

Some bacterial or viral infections can give rise to a cluster of psychological symptoms called a **syndrome**. For example:

- Untreated syphilis infection can lead to a condition called 'general paresis'. This condition leads to progressive paralysis and dementia as it affects the brain and spinal cord (the central nervous system). It is rarely seen today, as syphilis can be effectively treated with penicillin.
- More recently, Brown *et al.* (2004) have suggested that 14 per cent of schizophrenia cases can be linked to exposure of the foetus to influenza in the first trimester of pregnancy.

Genetic factors

The more genetically similar people are, the more likely it is that they will develop similar mental disorders. Geneticists test this using family, twin and adoption studies to try to tease out the contribution of heredity and environment to psychopathology. For example, Zimbardo *et al.* (1995) found that, in genetically identical (monozygotic or MZ) twins, the concordance rate for schizophrenia was 48 per cent, while in non-identical (dizygotic or DZ) twins it was 17 per cent. Since each member of a twin pair grows up in a shared environment, the difference in genetic resemblance is argued to be the only way to account for that difference.

Biochemistry

Some forms of psychopathology involve imbalances in biochemicals known as **neurotransmitters**, whose role it is to transmit messages between the nerve cells (neurons) that make up the nervous system. Similarly, imbalances can occur in the endocrine system, which secretes biochemicals in the form of **hormones**. For example:

- Lowered levels of the neurotransmitter serotonin have been connected with depression.
- Raised levels of the neurotransmitter dopamine are linked to schizophrenia.
- Cortisol (a hormone) increases dramatically when someone is stressed.

Evidence from PET scans, which can track neurochemical pathways in the brain, supports a biochemical explanation of some forms of psychopathology (Mann *et al.* 1996), but the reason for an imbalance is not always well understood; genetic and environmental influences may both have a role to play.

Essential notes

General paresis can appear up to 20 years after contracting syphilis, so its cause proved difficult to detect until Noguchi and Moore (1913) used advances in medical technology to connect the presence of syphilitic spirochaetes (bacteria with a distinctive spiral shape) in the brains of people with this condition.

Essential notes

The concordance rate refers to how likely it is that a person with a mentally ill relative will develop the same condition. In identical twins, a 48 per cent concordance rate for schizophrenia means that, if one twin has it, there is a 48 per cent chance that their co-twin will also develop it.

Brain damage

Biological psychologists see the brain as central to behaviour. If there is a problem with its development, or if it malfunctions or is damaged, psychopathology might result. Conditions such as Alzheimer's disease are thought to be due to deterioration of the brain and its functioning, resulting in symptoms of dementia. Injury or poisoning can also cause brain damage; for example, Korsakoff's syndrome is related to alcohol abuse and leads to memory disturbances, confusion and apathy.

Evaluation of the biological approach to psychopathology

Good scientific support

The scientific nature of much of the evidence for causes of psychopathology is a strength of the biological approach. There is good scientific evidence from epidemiological and physiological studies to support the role of infection, genetics, biochemicals and brain damage in psychopathology. This means that the reliability and validity of findings are high.

Humane and effective treatments

Strong links with psychiatric medicine and the development of effective treatments lend further credibility to this approach. Advances in psychiatry have led to much more humane and effective treatment of the mentally ill. As the biological approach sees the body as the root of psychopathology, the individual is not usually seen to be responsible for any resulting behaviour that is damaging to themselves and others around them. Instead, they are seen as someone who can be helped.

Stigma

Biologically based approaches to psychopathology favour the use of classification systems, such as the Diagnostic and Statistical Manual of Mental Disorders (DSM), which involves labelling an individual as mentally ill. For some people, having a condition identified can be a relief from uncertainty. However, a label can carry a **stigma**, marking people out as diseased or disgraced, and this can lead to rejection, fear or avoidance by others. Antipsychiatrists such as Szasz, Laing and Goffman, writing in the 1960s, warned that labelling also encourages others to see the mentally ill as scapegoats and treat them accordingly. Recent initiatives to raise awareness of mental health issues among the general public can help to reduce such prejudice.

Biological reductionism

For many, the simplicity of the explanation of psychopathology is one of its advantages as it tries to reduce complex behaviour down to a physiological level. However, for some this is too simplistic: seeing an individual as a malfunctioning biological machine disregards the complexity of the whole person, for whom treatment on a number of different levels may be needed.

Examiners' notes

The success of biological treatments for abnormality can be elaborated by citing scientific research studies that actually demonstrate the effectiveness of biological treatments. Do your own research on this and make a *brief* point relating to whatever you discover.

Essential notes

The use of systems such as DSM is contentious in itself, as they may be culturally biased and have problems with reliability and validity.

Essential notes

The psychodynamic approach incorporates a family of approaches to psychopathology all based on Freud's psychoanalytic theory. Other approaches, such as those of Jung, Erikson and Klein, continued to share some of psychoanalytic theory's original assumptions but often with a change of emphasis.

Essential notes

The superego has two parts: the conscience, which makes you feel guilt if the ego fails to control the id, and the ego-ideal, which makes you feel good if the ego deals with id impulses in a socially acceptable way.

Examiners' notes

A note of warning: avoid the temptation just to list Freud's stages of personality development in your answers (as many students do). You must make any description of Freud's psychosexual stages relevant to psychopathology in order to gain marks.

Psychological approaches: psychodynamic

Basic assumptions of the psychoanalytic approach

Sigmund Freud (1856–1939) was the creator of psychoanalytic theory and hence the first psychodynamic approach to personality. He proposed that:

- much of our behaviour is biologically determined by the operation of unconscious instinctive forces residing in the **id** (see below)
- personality develops in stages, and what happens at each stage is vital in shaping personality
- early experiences, particularly in the first six years of life, profoundly affect later personality.

The structure of the personality
The adult personality consists of an id, **ego** and **superego**.

- The id focuses on pleasure and prompts behaviours that are infantile, basic and selfish, e.g. sexual impulses and aggression. Personality consists entirely of id until about 1½ years of age.
- The ego focuses on reality; it is able to delay gratification, encouraging the id to wait until the timing is appropriate. The ego is the adult voice of reason and emerges between 1½ and 3 years of age.
- The superego is the moral part of the personality, and arises from learning what is right and wrong. It is like an inner parental voice and emerges between 3 and 6 years of age.

Psychosexual stage of personality development
According to Freud, everyone's personality develops through a series of age-related, psychosexual stages. At each stage, the id focuses its pleasure seeking on a particular **erotogenic zone** of the body. The stages are:

- *The oral stage* (0–1½ years) – Pleasure is gained from oral comfort such as sucking and feeding.
- *The anal stage* (1½–3 years) – Pleasure is gained from expelling or retaining faeces. The ego develops in this stage.
- *The phallic stage* (3–6 years) – Pleasure is gained from the genitals. The superego develops in this stage.
- *Latency* (6 years to puberty) – A period of relative calm, focusing on social development.
- *The phallic stage* (from puberty onwards) – The personality is fully formed and pleasure comes from mature sexual relationships.

The origins of psychopathology

Conflict between the id, ego and superego
The id, ego and superego are in constant, unconscious, dynamic conflict with each other, so it is important that they are well balanced. The ego should be strong enough to satisfy the urges of the id in a way that the superego regards as socially acceptable. If the ego is weak, it could be overwhelmed by the id or superego.

The concept of anxiety is the key to understanding psychopathology. It is normal to feel anxiety about real dangers, but we can also experience other kinds:

- *neurotic anxiety* – resulting from conflict between the id and ego
- *moral anxiety (guilt)* – resulting from conflict between the ego and superego.

If the id threatens to overwhelm the ego, strong feelings of anxiety result, and if the ego fails to control the id, the superego induces guilt. These may be powerful enough to trigger anxiety disorders such as phobias and obsessive-compulsive disorder. However, the ego has a battery of emergency measures it can use to protect itself from anxiety, called **ego defence mechanisms**. These include:

- *repression* – pushing unacceptable urges into the unconscious mind
- *sublimation* – allowing socially acceptable expressions of an unacceptable urge such as aggression in a symbolic way (e.g. through a contact sport).

Fixation of psychic energy in the psychosexual stages

If an individual's eroticism is over- or underindulged at any of the first three psychosexual stages, psychic energy can become fixated (trapped), leading to an unbalanced adult personality. Fixations may be oral, anal or phallic – for example, a person with retentive tendencies, fixated at the anal stage, may become obsessed with orderliness or hoarding.

Evaluation of the psychodynamic approach

Determinism

Freud believed that our behaviour was determined, not only by unconscious, instinctive forces (**biological determinism**), but also by experiences in childhood (**environmental determinism**). Both normal and abnormal behaviour are thus **overdetermined** (have multiple causes). This could lead to people feeling they have very little free choice over how to behave and blaming their shortcomings on their parents; in other words, they may feel helpless instead of taking personal responsibility for changing themselves.

Difficulties with testing

Psychology is a science and therefore prefers to use empirical (publicly observable) data. The unconscious mind is not directly observable, if at all, so does not lend itself to scientific testing. However, not all psychologists agree that scientific method is the only way to gather knowledge. Some regard it as reductionist and, instead, value the depth of Freud's qualitative, case study-based observations, arguing that these give us detailed and wide-ranging understanding of individuals' experiences.

Influence on psychotherapy

Although Freud's theory has its critics, it could be argued that, without him, talk-based therapies such as counselling would not be as widespread as they are today, leaving many people with much more limited treatment options.

Essential notes

Some ego defence mechanisms are unsuccessful in that they fail to deal healthily with anxiety – e.g. repression simply pushes the problem into the unconscious mind, and displacement uses a scapegoat. Other defence mechanisms are successful in that they allow socially acceptable expressions of an urge – e.g. anxiety arising from an anally fixated desire to smear faeces can be sublimated symbolically through art.

Psychological approaches: behavioural

Origins of psychopathology

Behaviourists view psychopathology as environmentally determined, learned behaviour. Learning occurs in three key ways: **classical conditioning**, **operant conditioning** and **social learning**.

Classical conditioning

Pavlov (1927) demonstrated classical conditioning in experiments with dogs. He retrained their innate (unconditioned) salivary reflex to food by pairing food with the sound of a buzzer in several learning trials. Eventually, salivation was elicited by the sound of a buzzer alone. This model can explain how humans develop fears, phobias and other emotional reactions to previously neutral stimuli. They become associated with an innate reflex response, such as aversion to pain or physical reaction to pleasure.

Figure 4 shows how 11-month-old Little Albert was classically conditioned to fear a white rat (Watson and Raynor 1920). They banged a metal bar behind Albert's head, startling him, while presenting him with a white rat on several occasion. Afterwards, whenever Albert was shown the rat, he seemed fearful and tried to get away from it. The fear also generalized to objects resembling the rat, such as a rabbit, cotton wool and Watson's hair.

Operant conditioning

Skinner (1974) proposed a form of learning called operant conditioning, in which the frequency of certain behaviours can be changed by their consequences:

- Behaviours followed by rewarding consequences, bringing us pleasure (positive reinforcement) or escape from pain (negative reinforcement), tend to *increase* in frequency.
- Behaviours followed by unpleasant consequences (punishment), or no consequences at all, tend to *decrease* in frequency.

A phobia, for example, might be established by classical conditioning, but maintained by operant conditioning, in that the anxiety felt on encountering the phobic object can be reduced, and thus negatively reinforced, by running away from it. Conversely, depressive behaviour might be positively reinforced and thus maintained by the care and attention it elicits from others.

Fig. 4
Classical conditioning of rat phobia

	Stimulus		Response
Unconditioned reflex	Unconditioned stimulus (UCS)	⟶	Unconditioned response (UCR)
	Loud noise		Startle to loud noise
Conditioning trials	CS	+ UCS ⟶	UCR
	White rat	+ Loud noise	Startle to loud noise
Conditioned reflex	CS	⟶	Conditioned response (CR)
	White rat		Startle

Social learning theory (SLT)

Bandura's (1973) SLT proposes that we learn from watching the behaviour of others. We internalize their behaviour but only perform it ourselves if the person modelling it is significant to us and its consequences seem good for them. A child could learn a phobic response from observing a parent reacting with fear to something such as a dog, internalizing the fear and reproducing it next time a dog is encountered. Mineka *et al.* (1984) demonstrated that fear of snakes (ophidiophobia) could be learned by infant monkeys from their parents. The ability to learn behaviour this way makes evolutionary sense if it is good for our survival.

Evaluation of the behavioural approach

The behavioural approach has many of the characteristics of science, and this can be seen as both a strength and a weakness.

Empirical research support

Behaviourists emphasized testing empirically observable behaviour in a scientific manner, usually in the laboratory and with an emphasis on experimentation. Cases such as that of Little Albert and extensive animal research by Skinner, among others, have given this approach good research-based backing. The effectiveness of behavioural treatments for certain disorders also validates this approach (see pp. 60–4).

Determinism

Behaviour, whether healthy or unhealthy, is seen as being environmentally determined. One consequence of this is an ethical one: people with disorders are not seen as responsible for their condition and, therefore, should not be stigmatized. Another consequence is the optimistic view that psychopathological behaviour can be unlearned and is thus controllable. On the other hand, this underplays the amount of free will and choice that people can exercise over their behaviour – factors that could play an important part in recovery.

Reductionism

This approach can be criticized for its emphasis on overt behaviour, failing to consider the whole person and complexity of certain psychopathologies. Not all psychopathology is this easily explained (e.g. schizophrenia), so focusing on behavioural symptoms alone could mean that other underlying causes are not treated. A less simplistic explanation is sometimes necessary.

Parsimony

Science favours parsimonious (economical) explanations of behaviour, and behaviourism can explain the origins of some psychopathologies very clearly. A good example of this is the case of Little Albert, whose fear of rats was neatly explained by classical conditioning. Similarly, Little Hans' fear could be simply explained as resulting from being frightened by a horse rather than from an unconscious fear of his father (see p. 58). However, parsimonious explanations may not always be complete; for example, some classically conditioned associations are learned more rapidly than others, which suggests that there is a biological basis to phobias as well.

Psychological approaches: cognitive

Cognition and psychopathology

The cognitive approach to psychopathology comes in various forms, but all of them see psychopathology as resulting from faulty cognitions about ourselves, others and our worlds. Such cognitions distort a person's reality and lead them to feel worthless, unhealthy, unhappy and unrealistic about the future. Two prominent theorists are Ellis (1962), who focused on irrational thinking, and Beck (1976), who focused on cognitive errors.

Irrational thinking (Ellis 1962)

Ellis states that the way we behave depends on how we think about something. For the most part, people are content and functional because most of their thinking and behaviour is rational, but we are also all capable of irrational thinking. Ellis felt that problems can arise when this becomes automatic and habitual, leading to dysfunctional changes in behaviour that make the person's life, or the lives of those around them, difficult. Several types of irrational thinking are illustrated in Table 5.

Errors in logic and the cognitive triad (Beck 1967)

Beck (1967) agreed with Ellis that distorted thinking was the basis for psychopathology, particularly depression, which he suggested was a by-product of the following:

- *Errors in logic* – These errors are similar to the ones in Table 5 and concern the way in which someone construes an event in the past, present or future. For instance, someone might fail an exam, or anticipate failing one, and so conclude that they are stupid. The negative thinking that follows failure, or anticipated failure, lowers their self-esteem and has consequences for how they behave.
- *The cognitive triad* – The cognitive triad consists of three kinds of cognitive bias that depressed people tend to adopt. These are negative thoughts about the world, themselves and their future. These biases interrelate and tend to perpetuate someone's depression; for example, the individual might see the world as a generally hostile place in which they struggle to feel comfortable and which they will never be able to change. Figure 5 shows these three types of thinking.

Essential notes

Another cognitive explanation is the **information processing approach**, which views the person as a kind of computer and psychopathology as a malfunction in the system. Barch *et al.* (1999) proposed that a faulty attention system might be the basis of some kinds of schizophrenia in which individuals find it difficult to know what to attend to and feel overwhelmed with information or experience hallucinations.

Essential notes

People can give away their thoughts in the way they talk. Ellis identified the 'Tyranny of should, ought and must': for example, 'I should be a better parent', 'I ought to revise constantly', 'I must never show weakness'. If these standards are unreasonable or unattainable, they can lead to anxiety and/or unhappiness, which might become pathological.

Table 5
Examples of irrational thinking (Ellis 1962 and Beck 1967)

Type of irrational thinking	Description	Example
Catastrophizing	Wildly exaggerating the negative aspects of an event	'That exam was hard, so my future is ruined'
Polarized thinking	Seeing everything in extreme terms, as either 'black or white'	'He doesn't like me, so I must be a terrible person'
Overgeneralization	Drawing sweeping conclusions based on a single event	'He doesn't like me, so no one else does either'
Tyranny of 'should', 'ought' and 'must'	Expressing unrealistic beliefs or goals	'I must be loved by everyone'

Research support for a cognitive explanation

Rachman believed that obsessive-compulsive disorder was best explained by a four-stage process in the thoughts of a sufferer:

1. Obsessional thoughts occur – 'There are germs everywhere.'
2. They are misinterpreted – 'They could kill me.'
3. High levels of anxiety are experienced – 'I could die at any moment.'
4. Compulsions occur – 'I have to clean everything.'

Rachman (2004) carried out a case study of a woman that lent support to this proposed thought sequence. She had obsessional thoughts around traces of bodily fluids (step 1), which she thought might give her disease and kill her (step 2), and this made her extremely anxious (step 3). She felt compelled to look out for and constantly check for any sign of bodily fluids, particularly blood, in her environment (step 4).

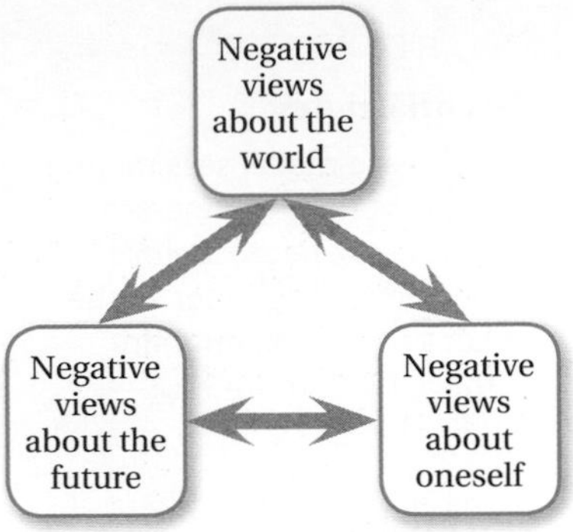

Evaluation of the cognitive approach

The importance of cognitions in therapeutic approaches

Behaviourists initially criticized cognitive psychologists for reintroducing unobservable mental processes into psychology, arguing that this moves away from the scientific ideal of using only publicly observable empirical evidence. Yet, cognitive-behavioural therapy (CBT), which has grown out of combining behavioural and cognitive approaches, is currently highly favoured. Alteration of cognitions is increasingly being recognized as an important element in a variety of therapies for a range of psychopathologies. If this is so effective, it could mean that the cognitive approach has validity too, either as a complete or partial explanation of conditions.

Cause or consequence?

Disordered thinking patterns are a feature of many mental disorders, but even Beck (1991) acknowledged that it is unclear whether they are the cause of psychopathology, a consequence, or both. In addition, they could be entirely causal in some conditions, or merely a contributory factor, or just a consequence. The success of cognitive techniques in treating psychopathology may, therefore, be the main contribution of the cognitive approach, as it may be that there is another explanation for its origin.

The question of individual responsibility

The cognitive approach to psychopathology works on the theory that thought processes are under the control of the individual. This is a mixed blessing: it is optimistic in that clients are thought to be able to bring about their own recovery (with therapeutic support), but it also holds them personally responsible for thinking in a dysfunctional way and bringing about their own problems.

While some psychologists welcome an approach that empowers the client in the therapeutic relationship, if the individual sees themselves as solely responsible for their condition, other causes that could be dealt with to good effect may be overlooked.

Fig. 5
Beck's cognitive triad of negative thinking

Examiners' notes

Using treatment as evaluation gives you the chance to show that you know about the treatment section of the topic as well as the explanations. It also has the advantage of being something you have to revise for the examination anyway.

Biological therapies

Biological therapies for treating psychopathology are based on the disease model, which believes that mental disorders can be treated as though they were physical illnesses. Two treatments are considered here: drug therapy and electroconvulsive therapy (ECT).

Drug therapy

Drug therapy, or chemotherapy, involves adjusting the neurochemical or hormonal imbalances thought to be involved in mental disorders by treating them biochemically, using three major classes of drug: anti-anxiety, antidepressant and antipsychotic drugs.

Anti-anxiety drugs

These are used predominantly for anxiety disorders and stress. An example is the minor tranquillizer Valium (diazepam), which is a benzodiazepine (BZ). BZs enhance the effects of the neurotransmitter GABA. This has a sedative effect on brain activity and calms feelings of anxiety (see p. 18).

Antidepressant drugs

There are three main types of antidepressant drugs: monoamine-oxidase inhibitors (MAO inhibitors), tricyclic antidepressants and selective serotonin reuptake inhibitors (SSRIs). These all work in different ways to alter neurotransmitter levels and improve mood. For example, low serotonin levels are associated with depression; MAO inhibitors block an enzyme that breaks seratonin down, thus prolonging its action. SSRIs work in a similar way by slowing the re-uptake of serotonin. Prozac is an example of an SSRI antidepressant.

Antipsychotic drugs

Antipsychotic drugs are used to alleviate symptoms such as hallucinations and delusions, conditions that feature in disorders such as schizophrenia. Their main function is to reduce the effect of the neurotransmitter dopamine but, because of the undesirable side effects of long-term use, 'second-generation' antipsychotics have been developed that work on other transmitters too. An example is clozapine, which reduces both dopamine and serotonin levels.

Combining drugs with cognitive-behavioural therapy (CBT)

In order to compare the efficacy of treatments for depression, Fava *et al.* (1998) randomly assigned 40 patients to drug therapy with standard clinical support or drug therapy followed by CBT. At a two-year follow up, 80 per cent of the drug group had relapsed, which was a similar figure to that found in studies that had used CBT and drugs, either alone or simultaneously. In comparison, only 25 per cent of the group using the drug followed by CBT had relapsed. The sequential use of drugs and CBT seemed to be critical in maintaining the improvements begun with drugs alone. Fava *et al.*'s (1998) study has, however, been criticized for its small sample size. The effect found needs to be replicated in order for it to be more widely generalized.

Essential notes

The disease model sees mental disorders either as illnesses with genetic, neurochemical or hormonal origins, or as the result of infection or brain damage (see pp. 48–9).

Essential notes

Any drug that enhances the action of a neurotransmitter is referred to as an **agonist**. Those that dampen activity by blocking or inhibiting neurotransmitters are called **antagonists**.

Examiners' notes

Using abbreviations (e.g. SSRIs, BZs) is acceptable when answering questions in this area, although it is better to use the full title *the first time* you refer to these in your answer.

Examiners' notes

You do not need to know all these different types of drugs, but knowing *some* helps you to avoid making sweeping generalizations about 'drugs' instead of specific points relating to specific types of drug.

Examiners' notes

The Fava *et al.* (1998) study is sufficient to learn in terms of research to support the use of drug therapy as a treatment. (You do not need to know one study for each kind of drug.) It could also be used as a supportive evaluative point.

Electroconvulsive therapy (ECT)

ECT is usually used on severely depressed patients who are unresponsive to drug treatment. It is also used for schizophrenia, alongside drug therapy. It involves administering a muscle relaxant and short-acting general anaesthetic, then inducing a brief seizure by passing a current between 70 and 130 volts through the non-dominant hemisphere of the patient's brain. There will typically be two to three ECT sessions a week for three to four weeks, depending on the severity of the condition and the patient's progress. The exact reason why ECT works is not known. It may be that it affects levels of particular neurotransmitters, resulting in an improvement in symptoms.

Research into ECT

Tharyan and Adams (2009) found that ECT is an effective treatment option for some people with schizophrenia. Results from 26 studies concerning almost 800 schizophrenic participants showed that treatment with antipsychotics and ECT was much more effective than antipsychotics alone and often better tolerated. It was also faster acting, which, in the case of suicidal patients, could be life saving.

Evaluation of drug therapy and ECT

Treating symptoms not cause

One of the main criticisms of drug therapies and ECT are that they just treat the symptoms. If a person stops treatment and relapses, it could be because there is a permanent biochemical problem, but it could also be due to factors in the individual's environment, such as a stressful home life, or even both (Hewstone *et al.* 2005). Treating symptoms, and not other possible underlying causes of a problem, might be overly reductionist.

Informed consent

The Mental Health Act (2007) emphasizes that drug therapy or ECT should be administered to patients with their informed consent wherever possible. In some cases, however, severe depression or a psychotic condition, such as schizophrenia, may make it difficult for the individual to understand what they are consenting to. In the case of ECT and some drugs, it is uncertain why they work, so even the clinician does not know exactly what patients are consenting to. A decision may have to be made in the patients' best interests that takes away their personal freedom to choose.

Side effects

All drugs have side effects. For example:
- Long-term use of some antipsychotic drugs can lead to movement disorders.
- Anti-anxiety drugs can cause drowsiness.
- Antidepressants can cause insomnia.
- ECT has been linked with long-term memory loss.

Some drugs also carry a risk of dependence. A decision needs to be made whether the benefits of the treatment – which can be considerable and rapid – outweigh the possible side effects.

Essential notes

Rose *et al.* (2003) found that 80 per cent of patients who received ECT were satisfied with the decision to have the treatment. This is an impressive figure, especially as ECT is used with severe cases in which the risk of suicide could be very high without treatment.

Examiners' notes

It is good practice in your evaluation to refer to other methods of treating abnormality to contrast with the one you are focusing on. For example, if the question requires you to outline and evaluate drug therapy, you can make the point about side effects in your evaluation, and then refer briefly to ECT, which also has side effects, then follow this by mentioning CBT, which is side-effect free. This shows that you not only know the treatment in question, but that you also know about alternatives.

Psychological therapies: psychoanalysis

Freud and psychoanalysis

Sigmund Freud's psychoanalytic theory attempted to explain many aspects of normal and abnormal human behaviour. He developed and refined it over decades along with its therapeutic application, known as psychoanalysis. Freud's psychoanalytic theory and practice were the first of a number of psychodynamic approaches, all of which are based on the concepts of the unconscious mind, the id, ego and superego, and instincts. Psychoanalysis was one of the first therapeutic techniques to use the 'talking cure' to treat anxiety-based neuroses.

The aims of psychoanalysis

Freud said that neurotic symptoms had multiple sources, so successful treatment involved identifying all their causes. As the sources of the problem lay in the unconscious mind, analysis took time and skill, especially as the client's conscious mind would resist exposing unacceptable impulses and unconscious defences. Psychoanalysis had two aims:

1. *To make the unconscious conscious* – Freud believed that conscious **insight** into the unconscious roots of a problem, such as fixations and ego defence mechanisms, would free the psychic energy that was being used to maintain them
2. *To restructure the personality* – As anxiety was thought to result from the ego feeling overwhelmed by the id or superego, it was necessary to strengthen the ego and rebalance the three parts of the personality. As Freud (1923) put it: 'Where id is, there shall ego be'.

An example of psychoanalysis: Little Hans

Little Hans (Freud 1909) had a phobia of horses, which emerged during the phallic stage of his development. Freud thought that boys of this age had unconscious, Oedipal desires for their mother mixed with fear that the father might find this out. This caused Hans such intense anxiety that he displaced the fear of his father onto horses, which he then avoided (i.e. he used an ego defence mechanism). Freud tried to use Hans' father as analyst (see Essential notes), but eventually Freud met Hans just once to help him become consciously aware of his unconscious motivations. It was said that Hans made a good recovery and became a psychologically healthy adult.

Psychoanalytic techniques

Freud's case studies of his clients were carried out using clinical interviews. Clients would typically recline on a chaise longue while Freud sat out of their sight at its head. In this relaxed and semi-hypnotic state, clients could concentrate on expressing their thoughts.

Examiners' notes

Try to avoid the temptation of talking too much about Freudian theory or giving too much detail about the Little Hans study below. However, if you are making a methodological point about the methods used in psychoanalysis, then you can use Little Hans to make a fairly brief point about the reliance on case studies to gain insights into a patient's condition.

Essential notes

Most of Hans' 'therapy' was carried out via his father, who reported to Freud via correspondence; Freud then gave directions as to how to deal with the situation based on his interpretations of the father's reports.

Free association

We usually consciously censor our thoughts and try to express only those that are acceptable but, in free association, the client says everything aloud no matter how trivial, disconnected, offensive or nonsensical it might seem. The analyst then looks for patterns that might betray underlying unconscious conflict and offers interpretations to the client. On occasion, the client may recall an earlier memory or come to an understanding that is so clear that they experience emotional release known as **catharsis**. This releases trapped psychic energy and makes it available for healthy functioning.

Dream analysis: the 'royal road' to understanding the unconscious mind

Freud believed that when we dream, the id's instinctual urges are more freely expressed but the ego still disguises anything unacceptable or threatening using such techniques as symbolization. The client's account of a dream must therefore be interpreted to make its unconscious meaning conscious.

Transference

During analysis, the client will transfer (project) characteristics of significant others, such as parents, onto the analyst, and express repressed feelings towards him or her as though they were the parent. This can help to reveal unconscious feelings so that they can be dealt with constructively.

Evaluation of psychoanalysis

The original 'talking cure'

Freud was one of the first to use clinical interviews to treat psychological problems, forming the foundation of many other forms of therapy and counselling such as CBT (see pp. 62–3). Without psychoanalysis, we may not have the wide variety of psychotherapies that now exist and that have helped many people with psychological problems.

Effectiveness of psychoanalysis

Eysenck (1952) claimed that 70 per cent of people treated for neuroses by GPs recovered, compared to only 44 per cent of psychoanalytic clients. Bergin (1971), however, reassessed Eysenck's data and estimated that 83 per cent of people improved with psychoanalysis compared with only 30 per cent of untreated people on waiting lists. Given that there is such disagreement over how to assess therapeutic effectiveness, Kline (1984) argued that the main criterion should be client satisfaction.

Range of application

Fonagy (2000) found that psychoanalysis was consistently effective for people with mild neurotic disorders but not for more serious ones. However, regardless of the severity of neurosis, psychoanalysis may not be accessible to those who are not verbally articulate, so it is certainly inappropriate for psychotic conditions in which a person may have lost contact with reality and is unable to reflect on themselves or engage in discussion. This means that its range of application is limited to particular kinds of person and psychopathology.

Essential notes

These are just a few of the many techniques Freud used to uncover unconscious motivation; he would also analyse people's sense of humour, religious beliefs and parapraxes (Freudian slips of the tongue or pen).

Essential notes

Phallic symbolization is one example of dream work in which a penis might be replaced, for example, by a tower or a sword. Freud did not think all objects were symbolic, however. When asked about the symbolic significance of his own cigar-smoking habit, he is reputed to have replied that a good cigar was merely a smoke.

Essential notes

Freud (1895) was realistic about what therapeutic success meant. To one client he wrote: '...much will be gained if we succeed in transforming your hysterical misery into common unhappiness. With a mental life that has been restored to health, you will be better armed against that unhappiness.'

Essential notes

Critics of talk-based psychotherapy say they favour 'Young, Affluent, Verbal, Intelligent and Successful' (YAVIS) individuals (Schofield 1964) rather than people who are 'Homely, Old, Unattractive, Nonverbal and Dull' (HOUND). This would limit the applicability of the therapy and lead to research findings that cannot be widely generalized.

Psychological therapies: systematic desensitization

Theoretical background

Systematic desensitization, first named by Wolpe (1958), is a psychological therapy based on behaviourist theories of classical and operant conditioning. These view learning as the formation of stimulus-response (S-R) connections, most of which will be adaptive but some of which can be maladaptive. It is assumed that any kind of learned behaviour can be unlearned or modified by breaking or changing S-R connections and systematic desensitization uses counter-conditioning to achieve this. It is a gradual process with several stages, which are outlined next.

The process of systematic desensitization

Stage 1: Relaxation training

The client is first taught relaxation techniques. These might involve deep breathing, progressive muscle relaxation or visualizing calming situations. They can be tailored to suit individual clients and aim to enable them to take conscious control of their mental and physical state.

Stage 2: Hierarchy of anxiety-provoking situations

With the help of the therapist, the client then draws up a list of situations involving the object of the phobia and arranges them in a hierarchy ranging from the least to the most threatening. In treating arachnophobia (fear of spiders), for example, the client might construct the following list:

- seeing the word 'spider'
- looking at a photograph of a spider
- looking at a clear container with a spider inside
- picking up and holding the container
- watching the spider crawl out of the container
- holding the spider in the palm of the hand.

Stage 3: Reciprocal inhibition

To bring about desensitization, clients first use relaxation techniques to calm themselves. They are then faced with the first step of the hierarchy while trying to maintain a relaxed state. When they can do this, they systematically move to the second step and steadily continue in this way until they can relax in the face of their most feared situation. Achieving this may take a number of sessions. Desensitization is thought to occur because two opposing emotional states, such as panic and calmness cannot exist at the same time so, when emotions conflict, the stronger one prevails. This is called **reciprocal inhibition**: if calmness has the upper hand, fear must subside.

Research involving systematic desensitization

The case of Peter

Watson and Raynor (1920) demonstrated with Little Albert how animal phobias could be classically conditioned (see p. 52), but it was a

see p. 52

Examiners' notes

This theoretical background is included to help you to understand how and why systematic desensitization works. Use this information sparingly and tailor the content in any exam question to fit the exact requirements of the question. For example, the question on p. 86 requires an answer focused on the technique of systematic desensitization. The 'Strong answer' on that page shows how to focus on this in a highly effective manner without including less-relevant background material (as the 'Average answer' has included).

Essential notes

You can use the hierarchy of anxiety-provoking situations with many phobias. The idea is that they become steadily more challenging for the client. Sometimes it may be necessary to use in vitro desensitization, where the client imagines encountering the object they are afraid of or anxious about. An example would be imagining climbing up a high ladder with someone who is afraid of heights.

psychiatrist, Mary Cover Jones (1924), who showed how it could be treated. Although the term systematic desensitization did not exist at the time, her treatment of 3-year-old Peter was clearly an example of its efficacy. Peter, like Little Albert, had a phobia of white rats and furry objects but was particularly averse to white rabbits. He was too young to be trained in relaxation or to draw up a hierarchy of feared situations so, instead, Jones used a situation when Peter was naturally relaxed – in this case, when he was sitting in his high-chair eating a food that he liked. At first a caged rabbit was gradually brought towards Peter. Over time, the rabbit was freed and brought closer. Peter was eventually encouraged to touch it until, finally, he could play affectionately with it. When subsequently tested with other creatures, such as a mouse and worms, Peter's tolerance was much improved.

Evaluation of systematic desensitization

Does it deal with the underlying problem?
If maladaptive behaviour is learned, reversing that learning should eradicate the problem at source. However, psychoanalysts argue that it is simply blocking an outlet for underlying anxiety, which must then find another form of expression. This so-called **symptom substitution** is notoriously difficult to test, however, and has never been convincingly demonstrated, suggesting that systematic desensitization does deal with the source of a problem (Tryon 2008).

The issue of time
Systematic desensitization has to be carefully paced over several sessions, which takes time. **Flooding** (implosion) is an alternative behaviourist treatment which treats problems by exposing the person to the feared stimulus straight away. A gentler option is **graded exposure**, in which the individual faces a hierarchy of feared situations (but without the use of relaxation techniques). In both cases they find their own ways of coping. These techniques should be applied with care to carefully selected individuals as there is a risk that they could make matters worse.

It will only work with some people
Using the *in vivo* method, where the client actually faces the object or situation, is reported as having a higher success rate than the *in vitro* method. For example, Ultee *et al.* (1982) demonstrated this in desensitizing children who wouldn't swim because of a fear of water.

It is sometimes necessary to use the *in vitro* form of systematic desensitization, e.g. if the client is very young. This requires the client to imagine feared situations, but this treatment is only successful if the client has a good imagination. Without this, the therapist will struggle to desensitize the client.

Essential notes

Peter's treatment was sometimes carried out when he was in the company of other children, all of whom had been carefully selected because they were completely fearless of rabbits. This must have introduced a modelling effect which, in addition to the desensitization, would have helped Peter to overcome his fear. See p. 53 for a discussion of social learning.

Examiners' notes

Case studies such as that of Peter can be used to evaluate systematic desensitization because it shows how successful it can be as a treatment.

Examiners' notes

Contrast the slow process of systematic desensitization with drug therapy, which acts quickly. CBT (see pp. 62–3) also takes time to work, so you could mention this as a comparison with systematic desensitization in any exam answer that requires AO2 commentary.

Psychological therapies: cognitive-behavioural therapy

Theoretical background

Essential notes

CBT is an umbrella term for a number of therapies all of which have two elements – cognitive and behavioural – that they might emphasize to varying degrees.

Cognitive-behavioural therapy (CBT) combines elements of the cognitive and behavioural approaches to treating psychopathology. It works on the idea that our cognitions, or thought processes, shape the way we feel and this affects how we behave. While we are all capable of construing the world in faulty ways, if this becomes habitually irrational or negative it may eventually lead to psychopathological conditions such as anxiety or depression and the associated dysfunctional behaviour.

Examiners' notes

You will already have met a cognitive-behavioural therapy on p. 20 in the form of SIT (stress inoculation training). SIT is used mainly to deal with stress rather than abnormal behaviours, so is less relevant here than the two types of therapy included on pages 60–3. Stick to these, then, when answering questions on abnormal behaviour.

The cognitive element

The therapist helps the client to become aware of the nature of their thinking and the aspects of it that are causing problems. The therapist does this by careful and thorough questioning about the client's thoughts, ideas, attitudes, feelings and behaviour about themselves, others and real or imagined situations.

The behavioural element

The therapist and client work together to test and challenge the client's thought processes. They can test the connection between existing thoughts and behaviour in role play or in reality and then find alternative, more constructive ways of thinking and behaving. These new strategies can then be tested out both in a therapeutic setting and set as 'homework' for the client to try out in everyday life. Progress is paced to suit the client so that they gradually gain in confidence.

Therapeutic sessions are typically weekly or fortnightly and may last from about six weeks to six months depending on the severity and complexity of the problem.

A: Activating event
Example: A friend passes you in the street but doesn't say 'Hi'

↓

B: Beliefs (about A)
Negative: 'He's deliberately ignoring me.'
Alternative: 'He must be preoccupied or in a hurry'

↓

C: Consequences (of B)
Puzzlement, leading to either…
Negative: 'I will ignore him in future'
= *alienation from a friend*
Alternative: 'I'll call him to say hello and see if he's OK'
= *resolve*

Fig. 6
Ellis' ABC model of therapy

Examples of types of CBT

Rational emotive behaviour therapy (REBT)

Ellis (1962) proposed the ABC model to account for how psychological problems emerge and used it to help people to change their thought processes (see Fig. 6).

A negative event, such as apparently being ignored by someone you know, could be irrationally construed as deliberate rejection, which could lead to emotional upset and avoidance of that person in the future. A more rational way of thinking could be to assume the person was preoccupied or in too much of a hurry to stop and talk. Replacing irrational thoughts with rational thoughts such as these should lead to a more positive emotional reaction and more sociable behaviour. Ellis claimed that rational thinking could become a way of life leading to long-lasting improvements in the way someone thinks.

Beck's cognitive therapy

Beck *et al.*'s (1985) cognitive therapy was designed specifically for sufferers of depression, whose thoughts seem to revolve around negative thoughts about themselves, the world and the future. It encourages clients to monitor negative thinking, decide whether it is irrational, and, if so, to challenge it with more positive thinking. Beck later applied this technique to anxiety-based disorders, such as phobias, and to personality disorders.

Meichenbaum's stress inoculation training (SIT)

Stress inoculation training (SIT) is also a form of CBT and has been described and evaluated as a stress-management technique on p. 20.

Evaluation of CBT

The nature of the therapeutic relationship

Although psychotherapies, such as psychoanalysis and behaviour therapy, require the cooperation of the client, the therapist is the expert and tends to be in control of the process. CBT is collaborative with a more equal balance of power between the therapist and client. Clients are empowered to bring about their own recovery and equipped with techniques to maintain it. This is seen as more ethically acceptable than treating them as passive recipients of expert help.

Time-consuming treatment

CBT requires time and persistence on the part of the client, which may not suit everyone. Some individuals may not have the necessary motivation to complete the treatment, especially if they are so depressed that they struggle to get through the day. However, therapists argue that, although the therapy may not work as quickly as drug treatment can, it has no undesirable side effects and could be a more acceptable long-term solution. Fava *et al.* (1998), for example, showed that it can be used after swift-acting drug therapy to bring about a longer-lasting improvement (see p. 56).

Wide appeal

As well as being successfully applied in clinical settings, the accessibility of CBT principles means that they can sometimes be used by sufficiently motivated individuals to help themselves. For example, in his book, *Stop Thinking, Start Living*, Carlson (2003) explains how continually ruminating about negative things in life can lead to a depressed state of mind. He says there is no need to deal directly with negative thinking. Instead, he recommends concentrating on positive mental states whenever they are experienced so that they become more habitual than negative ones, leading to an overall improvement in mood.

Examiners' notes

In an exam answer it would be good to contrast CBT with drug therapy, which, it is argued, does not always resolve the problem at source. You could also mention systematic desensitization, which also endeavours to treat the problems not the symptoms.

Examiners' notes

Another way you could evaluate CBT is to show that it has empirical support and is often a valuable addition to other treatments. The study by Fava *et al.* (1998) described on p. 56 would work well here.

Answering AS examination questions

AO1, AO2 and AO3

The AS examination assesses three 'assessment objectives' known as AO1, AO2 and AO3:

- **AO1** assesses your ability to recall and show your understanding of scientific knowledge – e.g. describing a theory, explanation or study.
- **AO2** assesses your ability to analyse and evaluate scientific knowledge – e.g. evaluating a theory in terms of research support or applying that knowledge to a novel situation.
- **AO3** is concerned with 'How Science Works' – e.g. explaining, interpreting and evaluating aspects of research methods.

Examiners' notes

On the AQA Unit 2 paper, there are 24 marks for AO1, 24 marks for AO2 and 24 marks for AO3.

Be prepared

It is impossible to prepare yourself for *every* type of question that might be asked in the AS Unit 2 exam, but you can give yourself the best chance of success by tailoring your revision to the specific demands of the question types suggested on p. 68. The next stage of preparation comes when reading the specific requirements of the exam questions in the actual exam. This is the stage where it is easy to make mistakes, so it pays to do this *very* carefully. Consider the following questions, all very similar but very different in their specific requirements:

- Outline *how* **one** research study has investigated the relationship between stress-related illness and the immune system.
- Outline what **one** research study has *found* concerning the relationship between stress-related illness and the immune system.
- Outline **one** research study that has investigated the relationship between stress-related illness and the immune system.

The first question requires *only* methodological and/or procedural details, and not findings/conclusions or evaluation. The second requires *only* findings/conclusions and not methodological and/or procedural details or evaluation. The third question can be answered with a combination of the material from these two variants or just the findings/conclusions.

Examiners' notes

When answering the essay questions (usually worth 12 marks), you should bear in mind that half of these marks are for AO1 and half for AO2. An effective way of making sure you stick to this is to answer in terms of four distinct paragraphs, with two of these being completely AO1 description and two completely AO2 evaluation. Each paragraph would be about 75–85 words for a 12-mark question, and proportionately less for the lower-mark questions.

AO1

Detail is important

AO1 assesses your ability to recall and show your understanding of scientific knowledge relevant to a specific topic area. When allocating marks for AO1 questions, examiners look for accuracy and *detail*. Adding detail to your answer gets you more marks, so always think about how you can develop your answer. As a general rule: for 1 mark, make one point; for 2 marks make two points; for 3 marks, make three points and so on.

Consider the following question:

> *Outline the main features of the sympathomedullary system.* [**4 marks**]

You might begin by identifying an appropriate study (e.g. the NICHD study), then adding about four distinct pieces of information (in order to distinguish a 4-mark answer from one worth 1, 2 or 3 marks).

Here is an example of a four-mark answer:

When a stressor is detected, the hypothalamus activates the sympathetic division of the autonomic nervous system (ANS) *(point 1)*. When the sympathetic nervous system is activated, the body is put into a state of physiological arousal. Heart rate and blood pressure increase and fats are mobilized in the bloodstream *(point 2)*. When the stressor has passed, the parasympathetic division is activated and the body is returned to its resting state *(point 3)*. The ANS also controls the adrenal medulla. When this is stimulated, adrenaline and noradrenaline are released into the bloodstream and these support sympathetic activation *(point 4)*.

AO2

The nature of evaluation

AO2 assesses your ability to analyse and evaluate scientific knowledge relevant to a specific topic area. Students can often become confused as to what to include in an answer requiring evaluation. Options include:

- examples of research that either supports or challenges a particular theory or explanation
- practical applications
- methodological points (especially in questions specifically about research studies)
- implications
- gender and cultural differences and so on.

Elaboration

When allocating marks for AO2 questions, examiners look for appropriateness and *elaboration*. One way of elaborating effectively is to use the 'three-point rule'. This involves:

1. *identifying* the critical point
2. *justifying* the point
3. *explaining* why this is good (or bad) for the theory or explanation being evaluated.

> **Examiners' notes: AO2**
>
> It is worth placing obvious 'tags' on your evaluation. For example, instead of just *describing* a supporting research study, preface your description with a phrase such as 'This claim is supported by research by... which showed that...'

Applying your knowledge

Some of the AO2 questions in this exam require you to 'apply your knowledge' to a particular context, such as asking you to identify which definition of abnormality best fits a pattern of behaviour described in the stimulus material. In response to a question of this type, you need to demonstrate two distinct skills:

- an awareness of the characteristics that go with each definition of abnormality
- matching these characteristics to the stimulus material and choosing the most appropriate definition.

Concentrating on just the former without contextualizing this material would significantly reduce the marks awarded.

AO3

For the AO3 questions, you will be given a brief description of a study (related to biological psychology, social psychology or individual differences) and then asked a number of short questions about it. Some of these require contextualization in your answer – e.g. '*What was the independent variable in this study?*' – while others do not – e.g. '*Explain one strength of the independent groups experimental design*'. In the former example, the important phrase is 'this study', because that indicates that the answer must be contextualized. Failure to do this would result in a much lower mark.

Both AS papers (Units 1 and 2) include additional AO3 questions that ask about the different *methods* psychologists use when carrying out research (e.g. '*How have psychologists investigated obedience to authority?*') In addition, you may be asked about strengths and weaknesses of these methods, plus associated issues of reliability, validity and ethics.

Example questions and answers with examiner comments

On the following pages you will find sample questions followed by sample average and strong answers, and also **tinted boxes** containing the comments and advice of the examiners. Answers refer to content within the revision section of this book and additional content, providing you with the opportunity to consolidate and extend your revision and research.

Examiners' notes: AO2

For example, if your criticism is that a study lacks ecological validity, this point can be elaborated thus:

'This study lacks validity (*identification*), because research by X failed to replicate the findings of Y (*justification*), which therefore means that the findings of Y's research cannot be generalized beyond the specific situation of that experiment (*explanation*)'.

Examiners' notes: AO3

Note that some research methods (i.e. AO3) questions do not require contextualized answers, e.g. 'Give one advantage of using a pilot study in research', so it pays to read the question very carefully before answering.

AS Psychology Unit 2: Biological psychology, social psychology and individual differences

Introduction to Example Paper 1

The Unit 2 paper is divided into three sections, each worth 24 marks:
Section A: Biological psychology (pp. 69–75)
Section B: Social psychology (pp. 76–81)
Section C: Individual differences (pp. 82–86)

Questions are of three general types:
Assessment Objective 1 (AO1) – description; knowledge and understanding.
Assessment Objective 2 (AO2) – evaluation, analysis and application of knowledge.
Assessment Objective 3 (AO3) – how science works, e.g. explaining, interpreting, and evaluating research methods, ethical issues, and so on.

Questions include short answer, stimulus material and one or more 12-mark questions requiring extended writing. Note that all questions are compulsory – you have to answer every question in every section.

Specific question types

- **Recognition type questions:** This type of question typically involves completing a table, labelling a diagram and so on. These questions appear quite easy (and they generally are) but you still need to be careful to follow the specific instructions of the question. It is easy to lose marks because you have not followed instructions.

- **Description questions:** These questions may be worth anything from 2 to 6 marks, with the number of marks indicating the depth required in the answer. It is useful to be familiar with the different injunctions used in these questions, with 'identify' requiring a simple phrase or statement whereas terms like 'outline', 'explain' and 'describe' require more elaboration. Descriptive questions do not require any evaluative content and any such material would not receive credit unless it is explicitly asked for in the question (e.g. *'Give two advantages of…'*).

- **Research methods questions:** Questions may be general (e.g. *'What is a pilot study?'*) or specific to a particular study (e.g. *'Why was a pilot study used*

in this investigation?'). Questions that include the word 'show' (e.g. *'Outline what one research study has shown about…'*) require findings and/ or conclusions only. Questions that include the word 'how' (or similar word)(e.g. *'Outline how one research study has investigated…'*) require methods/procedures only. If questions are not restricted to 'show' or 'how', then all aspects of a research study (or studies) are creditworthy.

- **Application of knowledge questions:** These questions require you to apply your psychological knowledge to a novel situation. It is important to make sure your answer is both psychologically informed and explicitly related to the problem outlined in the question stem.

- **Essay questions:** These are typically worth 12 marks, although other mark values are possible. Essay questions require an equal division of AO1 and AO2 material. In your answer booklet there will be space to plan your essay. There is no need to cross this out as the examiner may well find some credit in your plan if you run out of time.

Section A: Biological psychology

Question 1

Outline the main features of the sympathomedullary system. [4 marks]

- As this question is worth just 4 marks, you don't need to give a lengthy description of the sympathomedullary system. Reference to 'the main features' is simply a way of instructing you to offer a précis of the whole system rather than focusing on just one aspect of it.

- You should include a reference to the role of the sympathetic branch of the autonomic nervous system and the adrenal medulla.

Average answer

This pathway operates when the person comes across a short-term stressor – for example, if a bear jumps out in front of us, or we are attacked by a mugger. It works by the autonomic nervous system causing bodily changes to prepare the body for fight or flight. These include making the heart beat faster and a rise in blood pressure causing blood to be pumped to the muscles quicker. Adrenaline is also released into the bloodstream.

This answer makes some good, accurate points. For example, it does operate under conditions of short-term stress; it involves the ANS causing the heart to beat faster and causes higher blood pressure, and adrenaline is released. However, after ignoring stories of bears and muggers, there is very little detail left.

2 out of 4 marks

Strong answer

When a stressor is detected, the hypothalamus activates the sympathetic division of the autonomic nervous system (ANS). When the sympathetic nervous system is activated, the body is put into a state of physiological arousal. Heart rate and blood pressure increase and fats are mobilized in the bloodstream. When the stressor has passed, the parasympathetic division is activated and the body is returned to its resting state. The ANS also controls the adrenal medulla. When this is stimulated, adrenaline and noradrenaline are released into the bloodstream and these support sympathetic activation.

This answer is accurate, detailed and makes appropriate use of the correct psychological terms. There are no wasted words and, at around 90 words, this is an appropriate length for a 4-mark question.

4 out of 4 marks

Question 2

Carla is approaching some important examinations at college, but has come down with a bad cold, which makes it difficult to revise. She remembers getting a cold just before her January examinations as well, which puzzles her as she is normally very healthy.

Use your knowledge of psychology to explain why Carla tends to get colds just before important examinations.
[3 marks]

You would need to spot that this 'application' question has two distinct requirements:
- to show an understanding of the relationship between stress and the immune system.
- to apply this understanding to one particular situation (Carla's tendency to become ill just before exams).

Concentrating on only one of these would reduce your marks dramatically.

Average answer

Carla becomes ill before her examination because she is stressed. Stress has been found to make people ill, and increases the likelihood that people will get colds and flu. For example, research by Rahe found that people who experienced significant life events were also more likely to become ill.

This student does not specifically refer to the influence of stress on the immune system that this question requires, although there is some peripheral relevance to the claim in the second sentence.

1 out of 3 marks

Strong answer

Carla becomes ill before examinations because they act as significant stressors in her life, and research has shown that significant stressors suppress the immune system. As a result, as the examination looms, Carla's immune system works less efficiently and so she is less able to fight off infection, and so she becomes ill more easily.

This is an effective answer that gives a clear and accurate explanation of *why* Carla gets ill before examinations. There is a clear link between examinations, stress, immunosuppression and illness.

3 out of 3 marks

Question 3

Student volunteers were asked to complete a daily hassles scale, which scored the number of daily hassles experienced over the previous week. The same 10 students also completed a happiness scale, giving a rating from 1 (very unhappy) to 10 (very happy). The results were plotted on a scattergram, showing the correlation between the two variables (Fig. 1).

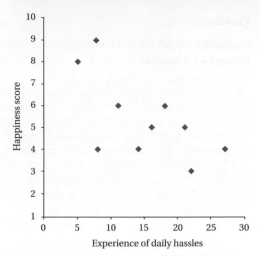

Fig. 1
Scattergram showing relationship between experience of daily hassles and happiness

Part (a)

*Give **one** conclusion that might be drawn from Fig. 1.* **[2 marks]**

- The most obvious conclusion that you might draw from this data is that there is a moderate negative conclusion between experience of daily hassles and happiness scores.

- A rule of thumb in 2-mark questions like this is try to give two 'bits' of information (i.e. 'moderate' and 'negative') and then put this conclusion in context (i.e. stating the two variables being correlated).

Average answer

There is a negative correlation between the two sets of scores.

A more complete answer would have included the fact that it is a *moderate* negative correlation. The student should also have referred to the particular variables under investigation rather than just stating 'between the two sets of scores'.

1 out of 2 marks

Strong answer

There is a moderate negative correlation between experience of daily hassles and happiness.

This has all the extra bits of information that were lacking in the 'Average answer', so would receive full marks.

2 out of 2 marks

Part (b)

*Give **one** strength and **one** weakness of correlations when used in the study of the impact of daily hassles.*
[2 marks + 2 marks]

- You are not being asked here to assess a strength and a weakness of correlational studies *in general* but when they are used in the study of the impact of daily hassles (e.g. on happiness). Therefore, you need to consider how any *general* strengths (e.g. ability to predict one variable by knowing the other) and weaknesses (e.g. inability to show a causal relationship between variables) might be particularly relevant in this research context.

- You are asked for *one* strength and *one* weakness, so providing more than one of each would be a waste of time and would earn you no extra credit.
- Because 2 marks are available for the strength and 2 for the weakness, you must provide some detail for each, i.e. not just state 'doesn't show a causal relationship'.

Average answer

A strength is that correlations are a quick and easy way to show the relationship between two variables.

A limitation is that a correlation can't show causality.

These answers should focus explicitly on the study of daily hassles, but the student does not mention this. Also, the student gives fairly superficial answers, though they would be worth a mark each. Both answers need development to get the second mark available.

1 + 1 = 2 out of 4 marks

Strong answer

Correlations allow the researcher to be able to predict one variable if they know the value of the other one. For example, if two variables have a strong negative correlation then they know that a high value of one variable should mean a low value of the other.

Correlations can only show that two variables are related, they do not show that one variable causes the other, which could mean that both are actually caused by a third variable.

This student offers an appropriate strength and an example that provides suitable elaboration to make sure of the second mark. You can use examples as a suitable way of adding elaboration if they make the meaning of an explanation (or as here, a strength) clearer.

The limitation is also appropriate and accurate. This time the student elaborates by discussing the implications of this problem (i.e. that a third variable may be involved).

2 + 2 = 4 out of 4 marks

Question 4

Outline what research has found about the relationship between personality factors and stress. **[6 marks]**

- You could answer this question by concentrating on just one type of personality factor associated with stress (e.g. Type A personality or the hardy personality) or both.
- For this 6-mark question, you would be expected to write about 120 to 150 words, so aim to balance depth and breadth, whichever approach you take.

- It is essential, however, to focus your answer on the *findings* of research rather than methodology.
- You should also focus on identifiable research studies rather than make a general statement about the relationship between personality and stress.

Average answer

Friedman and Rosenman (1974) believed that people with a Type A personality were always chasing deadlines and behaved with more hostility toward other people around them. To test this, they carried out an experiment, which looked at whether Type A personality led to more heart attacks. They interviewed 3000 men from California and tested whether they were Type A or Type B. Eight years later they checked up on them again and found that 70% of the men with Type A personality had developed heart disease. They concluded from this that having a Type A personality meant that people did not deal with stress very well, and that the stress had caused them to develop heart disease.

The description of the Type A personality is accurate enough although lacking in detail. The answer comes a little unstuck with the claim that 70 per cent of those with Type A personality had developed heart disease, which is just wrong (see the 'Strong answer' that follows, where the 70% figure is accurately used). The conclusion is appropriate, and rescues the impact of the earlier inaccuracy. With more detail and a little better attention to detail, this could have been a good answer, but as it is, this answer would only gain half the available marks.

3 out of 6 marks

Strong answer

Friedman and Rosenman studied 3200 men in the USA and identified the Type A personality. People who have a Type A personality tend to be extremely achievement oriented and respond with more hostility to stressful situations, and show an increased physiological response to stress, with increased heart rate and higher blood pressure. Friedman and Rosenman followed up these men 8½ years later, and found that 70% of those who had developed heart disease had the Type A behaviour pattern. Research by Kobasa *et al.* has shown that some people are more resistant to stress if they have a hardy personality. In a study of business executives, they found that these people tend not to get as stressed at work, seeing work more as a challenge than a stressor. Hardy personality types are more committed to their work and feel more in control, so don't get as stressed as people who are low in hardiness.

This student has included two appropriate personality factors: Type A/Type B and the hardy personality. There are two distinct research studies included to back up the descriptions and make the answer more authoritative. All the material is accurate and well detailed for an 'outline' question, and so this answer would be worth the full 6 marks.

6 out of 6 marks

Question 5

Hayley has always been interested in writing songs and performing them to her friends. However, she has been given the opportunity to perform at a prestigious London venue, and the possibility of other performances and even a recording contract. She worries about all the things that could go wrong and finds that as the date approaches she is becoming more and more anxious about it. In desperation she goes to her doctor who recommends a short course of stress inoculation therapy, which he feels would be particularly effective for her performance anxiety.

Part (a)

Outline what would be involved in stress inoculation therapy as it might be used to treat Hayley's performance anxiety. [**3 marks**]

- As with all 'application' questions, you would need to outline the main features of (in this case) stress inoculation therapy *and* place this understanding within a particular context (in this case Hayley's performance anxiety).
- Note that you don't need to explain what performance anxiety is or why it develops, only how the problem described in the stimulus material might be treated using stress inoculation therapy.

- The main phases of stress inoculation are conceptualization, skills training and application phase – you could explain each of these in the context of Hayley's performance anxiety.
- If you don't locate your answer in the context outlined in the stimulus material *or* you fail to provide the appropriate psychological underpinnings to any treatment of Hayley's anxiety, that would severely reduce the number of marks awarded.

Average answer

Stress inoculation therapy has three main parts. These are conceptualization, where the patient (Hayley) is encouraged to recall stressful situations and how they coped with them, and whether it worked. The second phase is skills training, where patients are taught relaxation and other coping techniques. The final phase is a real-life application where they put it all into practice.

The student has not put the answer into context, having only a brief reference to Hayley. The rest of the answer is a straightforward description of the technique rather than how the technique is relevant to Hayley's performance anxiety. It would not have taken much to turn this into a full marks answer, but without the required context it would receive a minimal number of marks.

1 out of 3 marks

Strong answer

In the first phase, conceptualization, Hayley relives similar stressful situations in the past (e.g. performing in a school play) and analyses whether her attempts to cope with the stress were successful. Next she would be taught various skills to deal with stress, e.g. relaxation techniques to keep her arousal down while performing or taught the link between practice and stress reduction. Finally she would put all these techniques into practice in a real performance.

This answer shows clear evidence of both requirements of this question. The accurate and detailed description shows clear understanding of stress inoculation therapy, and the student has located the answer explicitly in the context of Hayley's 'problem', elaborating the answer using specific examples that are clearly relevant to Hayley's situation .

3 out of 3 marks

Part (b)

*Outline **one** limitation of stress inoculation therapy as a treatment for stress.* **[2 marks]**

- It always pays to scan to the end of a question to see the number of marks allocated *before* beginning your response, as you could end up providing an unnecessary amount of detail. Sometimes this sort of question is worth 4 marks, sometimes 3 or, as here, just 2 marks.

- You should provide an appropriate amount of detail to match the number of marks allocated.

Average answer

A limitation of stress inoculation therapy is that it is very time consuming and expensive.

Well yes, SIT is time-consuming and can be expensive, but compared to what? Certainly not compared to psychodynamic therapies. Making claims such as these must be qualified, but this answer lacks the detail necessary for the second mark.

1 out of 2 marks

Strong answer

A limitation is that it may be time-consuming and would require a high level of motivation from the patient compared to other simpler techniques of stress management such as taking anti-anxiety drugs.

This answer is similar to the 'Average answer', *but* it offers the qualification that was missing in that answer (i.e. 'compared to   '). The limitation described is therefore accurate, appropriate and sufficiently detailed, so is worth both marks.

2 out of 2 marks

Section B: Social psychology

Question 6

Place the appropriate letter (from A to D) in the box next to the two definitions below of why people might go along with the views or behaviours of others.

A: Commitment

B: Compliance

C: Identification

D: Internalisation

To gain their approval or avoid disapproval ☐

Because of an acceptance of their views ☐

[2 marks]

- This question is designed to test whether you can really distinguish between the two different types of conformity detailed on the specification and whether you truly understand what each means.

- In order to prevent this being a 50:50 choice (where the right answer would be achieved 50 per cent of the time by luck alone), the question gives four options, out of which you need to make two choices.

Average answer

The student puts A in the first box and B in the second.

This appears to be guesswork, as the correct choice is B and D, and so gains no marks.

0 out of 2 marks

Strong answer

The student puts B in the first box and D in the second.

Both decisions are right, so this answer gains both marks.

2 out of 2 marks

Question 7

Amir's parents despair of his attitude to life. He does very little exam revision prior to his AS levels because he believes that whatever is to happen to him in the future is out of his hands and so there is no point in trying to change things by working hard.

Explain Amir's behaviour in terms of his 'locus of control'. [**4 marks**]

● This question assesses your understanding of 'locus of control' and your ability to use this understanding in the scenario outlined in the stimulus material. Doing one without the other would affect the number of marks awarded.

● You should identify that Amir appears to have an external locus of control, and then identify which aspects of his behaviour suggest this (e.g. facing stressful events such as exams with a passive and fatalistic attitude).

Average answer

Amir's locus of control means that he doesn't feel that anything he does will make any difference to what happens to him. This means that he doesn't feel that working is worthwhile, so doesn't bother. This means that he feels that whatever he does now won't improve his grades.

This student doesn't seem to understand what locus of control means, or that Amir's behaviour indicates that he has an external locus of control. Some of the answer is implicitly relevant to the question, but this is mostly a rewording of the information in the stimulus material.

1 out of 4 marks

Strong answer

Amir has an external locus of control. This means that he believes that whatever happens to him is controlled by external forces, which explains why he doesn't think it is worth working for his examinations. People with an external locus of control believe that things just happen to them regardless of what they do, so Amir may believe that 'fate' will intervene and decide his future. They also tend to face stressful situations (such as examinations) with a more passive attitude, which is probably why his parents get so annoyed with him.

This is a much stronger answer because it shows clear understanding of the characteristics of an external locus of control and applies this understanding explicitly to Amir's behaviour. For example, the student explains that people with an external locus of control face stressful situations with a passive attitude, which is probably why his parents get annoyed. Perhaps not quite enough detail for full marks, but clearly a very competent answer.

3 out of 4 marks.

Question 8

A psychologist would like to replicate Milgram's study on obedience to authority but the ethics committee reject her application, pointing out the ethical issues that would have to be addressed before any such replication was allowed.

Part (a)

*Identify **one** ethical issue in Milgram's original study and explain why this would be a problem for any attempt at replication.* **[3 marks]**

- There are two 'subparts' to Part (a) of this question. One mark is allocated for identifying the ethical issue (e.g. deception) and 2 marks for explaining why this would be a problem for any replication.

- You should give an informed and not speculative answer here, and phrase the second 'subpart' so that it focuses on replication of the study rather than Milgram's original study.

Average answer

Milgram has been criticized for causing his participants a great deal of stress by convincing them they were giving electric shocks to the learner. This also means that he was deceiving his participants and so they could not give their full informed consent.

This answer identifies *two* ethical issues (causing stress and deception), but only one can be credited. Probably the second is the better one, although as neither explains why this would be a problem for any replication, they fail to cash in on the fairly easy marks available. For instance, why would an ethical committee reject the use of deception in any replication?

1 out of 3 marks

Strong answer

Milgram was accused of causing psychological harm to his participants. This could have been caused by having to give potentially lethal electric shocks to other people or from pressure from the experimenter to continue when they were reluctant to do so. The BPS forbids causing psychological harm to participants, which is why replication would be difficult.

The student identifies the ethical issue appropriately and explains in detail the reasons *why* this is an ethical issue in Milgram's study. The answer also clearly explains the reason for it being a problem (in terms of the BPS guidelines forbidding exposing participants to conditions that might cause them psychological harm through stress). There is enough detail for the full 3 marks.

3 out of 3 marks

Part (b)

Outline how the researcher might resolve the ethical issue identified in Part (a) so she can make the possibility of her replication of this study more likely. **[3 marks]**

- There are 3 marks available for this 'subpart', so your answer should be appropriately detailed. As a rule of thumb, for 3 marks you should attempt to say three distinct things so that the examiner can easily distinguish between an answer that is worth 1, 2 or 3 marks.

- As before, there is an explicit requirement to focus on the replication rather than Milgram's original study. Therefore, you should focus on the ethical issue you identified previously and not on some unrelated issue.

Average answer

The researcher could lower the stress by making the procedures less stressful, for example by not putting the participants under any pressure to continue and allowing them to leave when they want.

This is a reasonable answer although a rather repetitive first sentence. However, the second sentence is better and offers an appropriate example of *how* the procedures could be made less stressful. Although 2 marks seems quite generous, this answer is clearly worth more than just a single mark.

2 out of 3 marks

Strong answer

She could omit the pressure to continue that was a feature of the original study and emphasize participants' right to withdraw at all times. She should also carefully screen all the participants so that nobody who takes part might potentially suffer as a result of participation in the experiment, for example by having a psychological condition that makes them vulnerable to the effects of stress.

This student has clearly thought about both the original experiment *and* how the ethical issue they previously identified might be reduced in any replication. This is an effective answer with an appropriate level of detail for the full marks available.

3 out of 3 marks

Question 9

*Outline and evaluate **two or more** explanations of how people might resist pressures to obey authority.*
[12 marks]

- This question is not an invitation to write a lengthy exposition of Milgram's obedience studies, but to use the insights from that study (and obedience research generally) to explain how people might resist pressures to obey.
- You could use many different explanations in response to this question, including the role of disobedient models (a key finding of Milgram's research), questioning the motives of the authority figure, and so on.

- The question asks for 'two or more' explanations, leaving it up to you, but you won't necessarily get more marks for more explanations. In fact, if you include too many, you could make your answer too superficial for high marks.
- As well as AO1 description, you need to include AO2 evaluation, and both should be equally well developed. For your AO2 evaluation, you could include a reference to Milgram's study to justify the choice of explanation, or reference to real-life events to show historical evidence of successful resistance.

Average answer

In this essay I will outline three different explanations of how people resist obedience, then I will evaluate each of these explanations. The first explanation is that people can resist authority when the authority figure is not physically present. Milgram found that when the authority figure gave their orders over the telephone, the participants were more likely to resist them. There is support for this from Milgram's study because participants often lied and said they were increasing the shock levels but then they just gave 15-volt shocks throughout. This shows that people are more able to resist authority when not physically present.

The second explanation is the presence of disobedient confederates. Milgram found in one variation of the study that when two confederates refused to go on giving shocks, then only a very small minority of participants continued giving shocks. This is because they had seen the confederates refuse and so they felt they could also refuse.

A third explanation is when people feel empathy for the victim. One participant claimed she had grown up in Nazi Germany and had to suffer all the hostility against Jews so she had no wish to inflict pain on another person. With this participant, even when the learner was ☞

in another room, she could not shock them because she could imagine what they must be feeling. This supports the claim that empathy for the victim is an important factor in resisting obedience.

First, there is no need for the 'In this essay I am going to…' introduction. It just wastes time and gains no marks.
- Description – The AO1 content is accurate and reasonably detailed, and would probably be worth 4 marks. More detail, perhaps explaining *why* each of these allows the individual to resist the tendency to obey, would have raised the mark awarded for AO1.
- Evaluation – Students may be surprised to have to offer AO2 evaluation in connection with 'explanations', but such questions are as likely as questions that ask for evaluation of a theory or research. This student has provided very little evaluation, other than perhaps the inclusion of the example to justify the importance of empathy in resisting destructive obedience. Because there is very little AO2, that can only be credited with a single mark.

4/6 marks + 1/6 marks = 5 out of 12 marks

Strong answer

Milgram found that his participants felt better able to resist the authority figure if there were disobedient role models present. These role models were able to provide social support for the participants who felt more able to resist because they were not alone. When confederates refused to continue delivering shocks, only 10% of the real participants continued to the full 450 volts. There is historical support for the important role played by disobedient role models in resisting authority. In the Rosentrasse protest against the arrest of their Jewish husbands during the Second World War, women protestors felt able to resist the Gestapo's orders to disband because they were in the company of other women who were also willing to resist authority and who provided social support.

A second explanation is that people with more advanced moral reasoning are more likely to resist authority if they feel that what they are being asked to do is considered immoral. Rosenhan (1969) carried out a replication of Milgram's obedience study. He found that those individuals who resisted the experimenter's pressure to obey based their decisions on more advanced moral principles (e.g. arguing that it was not acceptable to punish somebody just in the interests of completing an experiment) than those who obeyed, and who reasoned at a less mature level of morality (for example, believing that they had to obey the authority). However, a problem with this explanation is that people who are considered more moral are not necessarily less ☞

obedient. For example, Milgram found that adherence to religious values was not correlated with lower levels of obedience. Milgram actually found that Roman Catholics were more likely to obey than other participants.

A final explanation is when people question the motives and status of the authority figure. This prevents the sort of automatic obedience that Milgram found when carrying out the study in the prestigious surroundings of Yale University. To support this explanation, when the study was moved to run-down office buildings and the experimenter had less legitimate authority and expertise (as the experiment was no longer associated with the university), obedience levels dropped sharply.

This student has offered three distinct explanations (role of disobedient models, moral reasoning and questioning the motives and status of authority):

- Description – Each of these explanations is described clearly and accurately, with appropriate detail. Taken as a whole, the AO1 content would be worth the full 6 marks.
- Evaluation – The AO2 material is slightly less well developed. It is appropriate and has a good deal of elaboration, but perhaps not enough for full marks. The student has, however, made intelligent use of the AO2 'tags' (e.g. 'To support this explanation…'), and so this would be worth 4 marks for AO2.

6/6 marks + 4/6 marks = 10 out of 12 marks

Section C: Individual differences

Question 10

Part (a)

Outline the cognitive approach to psychopathology. **[6 marks]**

- This is a purely descriptive question asking you to outline the main assumptions of the cognitive approach to abnormality. You are not asked to include any evaluation here, so any AO2 material that wanders in to this answer would not receive marks.
- In order to get a decent balance of breadth and depth in your answer, you might consider making about four points, each of about 30 to 40 words. To do this, you will need to edit your writing tightly and not waste time on unnecessary content that would be unlikely to earn marks.

- You could appropriately include the role of irrational thinking and cognitive distortions, the ABC model and the cognitive triad. Use any examples to illustrate the approach sparingly, and certainly not instead of actual description of the approach itself.
- Although there is no requirement to include anything about the use of cognitive methods in therapy, you *could* mention the fact that one of the assumptions of this approach is that as irrational thinking is considered the underlying problem, then therapeutic intervention is also cognitively based.

Average answer

The cognitive approach claims that people with a mental disorder think differently to normal people. Ellis believed that everybody thinks irrationally at times, but sometimes these irrational thoughts can become abnormal. One way in which people can think abnormally was summed up in the ABC model. A is the 'activating event'. This is something in the person's environment e.g. the sight of a dog. B is the 'belief', which might be that the dog might attack them. This is an irrational way of thinking. C is the 'consequence', which might be maladaptive, e.g. avoiding all dogs or developing a phobia about dogs. The cognitive approach also believes that cognitive therapy is the most appropriate way of treating abnormality.

This answer is reasonably well informed in that everything included here is accurate and relevant to the question. It does, however, lack the level of detail associated with the highest-grade answers. The student could, for example, have developed their description of 'irrational thinking' or explained how or when commonplace irrational thoughts would be considered 'abnormal'. However, it is still worth more than half the available marks.

4 out of 6 marks

Strong answer

The cognitive approach argues that a person's thoughts and expectations influence their behaviour. If the person begins to think irrationally, then they may also start behaving in a way that is maladaptive, e.g. having negative thoughts about being worthless following a romantic rejection and so avoiding social contact. If these thought processes result in behaviour that goes against social norms (i.e. causing them to behave in a way that society considers abnormal) or interferes with their ability to lead a normal life, then it is considered psychopathological. Beck (1967) believed that negative thinking could lead to depression. He identified three forms of negative thinking called the 'cognitive triad'. This way of thinking is typical of people suffering from depression. This involves negative views about themselves (e.g. believing they are worthless), negative beliefs about the world (e.g. that everybody is against them) and negative views about the future (e.g. that they will never be good at anything).

At over 150 words, this is a very detailed outline of the cognitive approach, with all the points elaborated for greater impact. For example, the student elaborates 'thinking irrationally' by giving a suitable example of negative thoughts ☛

concerning romantic rejection. The student also works the 'cognitive triad' into the answer well, and by including examples for each of the three stages of the cognitive triad, they add the all-important extra detail. Everything here is accurate, so the answer would be worth the full 6 marks.

6 out of 6 marks

Part (b)

*Outline **one** strength and **one** limitation of the cognitive approach to psychopathology.* [2 marks + 2 marks]

- There are two requirements, one *strength* and one *limitation*. You could identify research support, therapeutic applications, etc. (strengths) or contradictory research evidence or cause/effect problems (limitations). Try not to be speculative when writing about the strength and the limitation, and use evidence where possible.

- Because there are 2 marks for each of the strength and limitation requirements, you should do more than just identify each of these (i.e. don't just say 'is supported by research'). However, as it is *only* 2 marks each, you should resist going into unnecessary detail once the 2 marks have been earned!

Average answer

A problem for the cognitive approach is that it only explains how people think, it doesn't explain why people think in that way, i.e. what has caused the irrational thinking in the first place.

Another problem is that it sees the problem as being inside the individual, i.e. they are responsible for their own irrational thought processes rather than it being a problem of the environment they live in (e.g. an unhappy relationship).

This student has made the mistake of providing two limitations rather than the required one strength and one limitation. In such situations, an examiner would read both and credit the better one. The student probably explains the second limitation better, so that would be the one credited. This would be worth 2 marks, but as there is no strength, the 2 marks available for that would not be awarded.

0 + 2 marks = 2 out of 4 marks

Strong answer

A strength of this approach is that there is research evidence to support its claims. For example, Gustafson (1992) found that many people with psychopathological disorders also displayed irrational thinking.

A limitation is that because of the focus on the individual's own irrational thought processes being responsible for their illness, it distracts attention away from the possibility of changing stressful social conditions that might lead to their mental disorder.

Unlike the 'Average answer', this answer gives a clear *strength* and a clear *limitation*. Each is appropriate, and the student suitably elaborates each one to a level that guarantees both of the marks available. For example, in the limitation, the answer gives the implication of focusing too closely on irrational thought processes alone.

2 + 2 = 4 out of 4 marks

Question 11

One way of defining abnormality is in terms of a person's 'failure to function adequately'. Jasmine worries that under this definition she may indeed be 'abnormal' as there are a number of areas of her life where she feels unable to cope effectively.

Part (a)

*Outline **two** characteristics that might persuade Jasmine that she may indeed be considered 'abnormal' under the 'failure to function adequately' definition.*

[2 marks + 2 marks]

- You could choose 'informal' characteristics, e.g. inability to take part in social activities, or 'formal' characteristics, i.e. a criterion from the Global Assessment of Functioning Scale (e.g. some impairment in reality testing).

- There is no evidence that Jasmine *does* have these characteristics, but you should imagine that you are advising her, and so don't leave her out of your response to this question!

Average answer

If she acts in a strange way (e.g. being very shy) or in a way that stops her living a normal life (e.g. not going out).

This answer gives two appropriate characteristics, but at a superficial level. It would have been better for the student to have separated each of these characteristics into distinct points and elaborated each in turn. Remember the rule of thumb: for 2 marks, say two things. The example given in brackets for each helps, but isn't quite enough to gain the second mark.

1 + 1 = 2 out of 4 marks

Strong answer

Two characteristics that might define Jasmine's behaviour as failure to function adequately are behaviours that are inefficient (i.e. doing things that are unnecessary), such as being unable to leave the house because of obsessions about locking the doors or switching all the lights off. Another characteristic is if she displays inappropriate social behaviours, such as not being able to carry on a conversation with another person or being excessively shy so that it becomes difficult to have a normal social life. This may convince Jasmine that she is becoming 'abnormal'.

The answer identifies two clear characteristics and gives appropriate elaboration *and* an example for each characteristic. This is an appropriate level of detail, and although the student hasn't given too much contextual detail, they have made sure to include Jasmine in their answer.

2 + 2 = 4 out of 4 marks

Part (b)

*Outline **two** limitations of the 'failure to function adequately' definition of abnormality.* **[2 marks + 2 marks]**

- To gain 2 marks for each of the two limitations, you should produce two distinct responses (perhaps separated physically so the examiner can see where one ends and the other begins).

- As examples of appropriate limitations, you could include the difficulty of distinguishing a 'dysfunction' from an abnormality, and the fact that what is considered 'adequate' functioning is itself open to question and subject to social and cultural factors.

Average answer

The 'failure to function adequately' definition can be criticized because it doesn't take into account cultural differences.

There is also a problem in determining whether something is just a characteristic of the individual or is a real abnormality.

As with the previous 'Average answer', this student has presented a fairly superficial coverage of two separate limitations. For example, the answer says that the 'failure to function adequately' definition doesn't take into account cultural differences, but does not say *why* this is a problem. The second limitation simply requires a little more clarification.

1 + 1 = 2 out of 4 marks

Strong answer

A limitation of this definition is that what is considered 'adequate functioning' may vary from culture to culture. This is a problem if the standards of one culture are then used to measure 'adequate functioning' in another, which results in an invalid diagnosis.

Some behaviours that might be classified as a failure to function adequately may actually help the individual to cope with life. For example, a person who displays some of the symptoms of depression may receive extra social support and attention from others.

Each of these limitations is clearly outlined and each comes complete with a second sentence that elaborates the identified limitation and secures the second mark available.

2 + 2 = 4 out of 4 marks

Question 12

Describe the use of systematic desensitization in the treatment of abnormality. **[6 marks]**

- This is an entirely descriptive question; therefore, you should not include any evaluative material in your answer. The command word is 'describe', so you should provide a reasonable amount of detail.
- You might include *why* systematic desensitization is used, the underlying principles of the therapy (classical conditioning) and *when* it is usually used (i.e. in the treatment of phobic anxiety).

- Although there is no set way of answering this question, there are some characteristics that an examiner would expect to see in an answer, including relaxation training, the hierarchy of anxiety-provoking situations, reciprocal inhibition of emotional states and possibly a distinction between *in vivo* and *in vitro* approaches.

Average answer

Wolpe developed this technique. He first locked a girl who was afraid of cars into a car and drove her around for an hour. Because nothing terrible happened during her car ride she was no longer afraid of cars. Wolpe went on to use this technique to cure people of phobias. First of all the therapist asks the person what it is that they are afraid of. With the patient they work out a hierarchy of fear, starting with something that causes them just a little anxiety and then working up gradually so they can face the thing that causes them the most fear. For example, if they are afraid of spiders they could start with a small spider some distance away, and then working up gradually to having a large tarantula on them.

This answer starts with an inaccurate description of Wolpe's original 'demonstration' of this technique, which is also unnecessary and would not receive credit. There is no mention of relaxation training, which is a crucial ingredient of this form of therapy as it works on the principle of incompatible responses (fear and relaxation). What is left is the hierarchy of fear and the gradual movement through this, for which the student would only gain 2 marks.

2 out 6 marks

Strong answer

Systematic desensitization is used as a treatment for the anxiety associated with phobias. A patient is first taught relaxation techniques because the treatment works on the principle that relaxation and fear are incompatible responses. The therapist and the patient then construct a desensitization hierarchy, which is a series of interactions involving the feared object, with each step in the hierarchy causing slightly more anxiety than the previous one. With the therapist's support and assistance, the patient then works through the hierarchy, starting with the stage that causes the least fear and trying to relax at the same time. When they can relax in the presence of that object, they work up to the next one, try to relax and so on. The technique can also be used with the patient imagining the feared object ('in vitro') rather than actually coming into contact with it ('in vivo').

At just under 150 words, this is clearly a detailed response to the question. Everything here is accurate and appropriate to the question. The student includes a description of why relaxation training is so vital, how the patient works through the hierarchy with the support of the therapist, and the difference between *in vivo* and *in vitro* treatment. This is a very effective description of systematic desensitization and would be worth the full 6 marks.

6 out of 6 marks

Average answers: overall

Looking at all the 'Average answers' to Example Paper 1, this set of responses has earned fewer than half the marks available and would probably earn the candidate a Grade C.

Strong answers: overall

Looking at all the 'Strong answers' to Example Paper 1, this impressive set of responses would clearly be worth a high Grade A.

Introduction to Example Paper 2

The Unit 2 paper is divided into three sections, each worth 24 marks:
Section A: Biological psychology (pp. 87–92)
Section B: Social psychology (pp. 93–97)
Section C: Individual differences (pp. 98–104)

Questions are of three general types:
Assessment Objective 1 (AO1) – description; knowledge and understanding.
Assessment Objective 2 (AO2) – evaluation, analysis and application of knowledge.
Assessment Objective 3 (AO3) – how science works, e.g. explaining, interpreting, and evaluating research
methods, ethical issues, and so on.

Specific question types
Questions include short answer, stimulus material and one or more 12-mark questions requiring extended
writing. Note that all questions are compulsory – you have to answer every question in every section. See the list
on p. 68 for a detailed description of the different types of questions that may be asked on this paper.

Section A: Biological psychology

Question 1

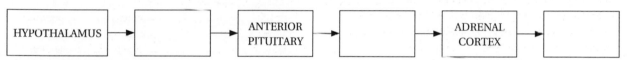

A: Adrenocorticotrophic hormone (ACTH)
B: Corticosteroids (e.g. cortisol)
C: Corticotrophin releasing factor

*The diagram represents the pituitary–adrenal system. Place the letter corresponding to each of the above points in
the appropriate place in the pituitary–adrenal sequence.* **[3 marks]**

- This question requires you to place letters in the appropriate box in the sequence. The letter C should go in the first empty box, the letter A in the second empty box and the letter B in the final box.

- Don't imagine that the examiner is being devious by making sure that none of the letters is in the correct sequence (i.e. the first box isn't A, nor the second B or third C). They just all happen to be like this because the three points are actually in alphabetical order!

Average answer

The student writes A, C, B.

A and C are the wrong way around, but B is in the right box, so just 1 mark for the correct answer.

1 out of 3 marks

Strong answer

The student writes C, A, B.

All three letters are in the right boxes, and so this answer gets full marks.

3 out of 3 marks

Question 2

Research has found that the physical environment at work (e.g. noise, heat) is a significant source of stress.

Part (a)

*Apart from the physical environment, outline **two** other sources of stress in the workplace.* [**2 marks + 2marks**]

- Don't be distracted by the context sentence that refers to the physical environment. In fact, you should *not* discuss any aspect of the stressful influences of the physical environment in your answer as the question explicitly *excludes* the physical environment.

- Suitable sources of stress include work overload, lack of control and role ambiguity. You must focus on the workplace as a source of stress rather than other stressors such as relationships, exams, etc. The question requires just two sources of workplace stress, so don't waste your time writing about more than two.

Average answer

A source of stress in the work environment is workload. A second source of stress is lack of control over the work.

This answer gives two appropriate sources of stress in the workplace, so it is appropriate *and* accurate. However, the student needed to elaborate, as well as identify, the sources of stress, to gain the second mark, for example, pointing out what it was about workload that made it stressful (e.g. presumably having too much work). Similarly, they might have explained the link between lack of control and stress. Remember, when there are 2 marks available, you should try to say two things to make sure of *both* marks. This answer would have gained only 1 of the 2 marks available for each stressor.

1/2 marks + 1/2 marks = 2 out of 4 marks

Strong answer

A source of stress is workload, i.e. having too much work to do in the time available, which results in people having to work long hours to try and cope.

A second source of stress is role conflict, i.e. having too many demands on their time (e.g. home and work), which causes stress as the person has to balance the demands of both roles.

This answer shows exactly how to construct an effective 2-mark answer. It clearly identifies, explains and elaborates each source of stress (i.e. explaining *why* each of these workplace stressors is 'stressful'). This would get full marks for each of the two stressors.

2/2 marks + 2/2 marks = 4 out of 4 marks

Part (b)

How have psychologists investigated the relationship between stress and the workplace? [**3 marks**]

There are two possible ways you could answer this question. You could describe:

- a general way in which psychologists study workplace stressors (e.g. the correlational method or longitudinal method), or
- the methods used by a specific psychologist or psychologists (e.g. Johansson *et al.* or Marmot *et al.*).

You should put your material into the context of the study of workplace stress rather than give a general description of method alone.

Whichever one of these approaches you take, you must focus on the *methods* used rather than the findings of research on workplace stress. You would gain 1 mark for describing the method itself, and the remaining marks for elaboration of the method within the context of workplace stress.

Average answer

Psychologists have generally used the correlational method. This involves measuring the amount of stress experienced and the level of the stressor (e.g. how much work they have to do and how stressed they feel).

The student has chosen a suitable method (correlational method) and given some fairly brief elaboration, which *may* just be enough to capture 2 out of 3 marks. To guarantee at least the second mark, the student might have explained a bit more precisely how this method has been used to 'correlate' workplace stressors and the experience of stress.

2 out of 3 marks

Strong answer

Research on workplace stress has made use of questionnaires, which measure the relationship between different aspects of the working environment and workers' experience of stress. Researchers have also used longitudinal studies, which measure the effect of stress over a period of time. For example, Marmot *et al.* (1997) carried out a three-year longitudinal study of civil servants, measuring the level of job control and the development of stress-related illness.

This student has presented two methods commonly used in the study of workplace stressors. Both are appropriate and the degree of elaboration offered is sufficient to guarantee full marks. The student has also avoided the temptation to write about the *findings* of Marmot *et al.*'s study (which would not have received any marks and so have been a waste of time).

3 out of 3 marks

Question 3

Part (a)

Outline what research has shown about the relationship between life changes and stress. **[6 marks]**

- This question identifies 'research' as a key requirement of the answer, so you should refer to one or more recognizable research studies.
- For 6 marks, you would normally expect to write between 120 and 150 words, so for this number of words you would probably write about the findings of more than one study.
- Note that the question asks you to outline what research has 'shown' rather than how the study was carried out. This is important because it means you will only get credit for writing about the findings of the study (or studies). Material on the methodology would not receive marks.
- You also need to be careful about the research you choose to include in any answer. Life changes are those major events in a person's life that cause significant transitions. They do not include, for instance, daily hassles or workplace stressors.

Average answer

Holmes and Rahe developed the SRRS, which measures the number of life changes (like marriage or the death of a spouse) and correlates these with the number of illnesses that the individual has experienced over the previous year. They found that the higher the score on the SRRS (life change units), the more likely they were to have been ill in the same period. Rahe *et al.* also used the SRRS to measure life changes and stress-related illness in American sailors and found that there was a positive correlation between stress and illness. Stone *et al.* (1987) asked married couples to keep a daily checklist of events in their life over a three-month period. They found that the number of undesirable events increased in the days just before a major illness.

This answer does include appropriate research studies (e.g. Rahe *et al.* and Stone *et al.*) but also includes some irrelevant methodological information from these studies. It is difficult not to assume that this is needed, but where it *isn't* needed, as here, it does not receive any credit. After stripping away the methodological content, the student has given only a fairly brief overview of results that is just about worth half the marks available.

3 out of 6 marks

Strong answer

Rahe *et al.* (1970) used the SRRS and found a small but significant correlation between the number of life change units experienced by sailors in the US Navy and their stress-related illness over a six-month period. This showed that experiencing significant life changes increased the likelihood of stress-related illness. Michael and Ben-Zur (2007) found widowed individuals scored higher in terms of life satisfaction before they were widowed than after, whereas with divorced individuals it was the other way around, they scored higher in terms of life satisfaction after their divorce than before. This was because more of the divorced individuals than widowed individuals were dating after their life change, therefore this had contributed to their increased life satisfaction. Lei and Skinner (1980) found that by adding up the number of events experienced (rather than using the weightings of the SRRS), this correlated as well with measures of stress-related illness as did the original SRRS score.

This is a very strong answer that presents three distinct studies related to life changes. Names and dates make this focus on specific research studies obvious, but there is no need to become anxious about getting the date wrong. There are no extra marks given for the correct dates, and so you can't lose marks for getting the date wrong. There is an excellent balance of breadth and depth in the answer, with all three studies clearly outlined and with an obvious focus on *findings* rather than methodology. This would receive the full 6 marks.

6 out of 6 marks

Part (b)

Sharon is undergoing a major life event (divorce), and is finding the experience extremely stressful. She goes to the doctor who suggests that drug therapy might help her to deal with the stress of her divorce and make her feel less anxious.

Identify a suitable drug that the doctor might prescribe to help Sharon deal with her stress, and explain how this particular drug would help her feel less anxious. **[4 marks]**

- This is an AO2 'Application' question, assessing your ability to *apply* your understanding of drug treatments. You would need to show that you understand drug treatments on anxiety (what they are, how they work, etc.) *and* that you appreciate how they might be used in the context of the stimulus material.

- Appropriate drug treatments include the use of beta-blockers, benzodiazepines and (possibly) antidepressants. Antipsychotics would not be relevant in response to this question.
- You would gain 1 mark for identifying an appropriate drug and the other 3 marks for explaining how the chosen drug works in this specific situation.

Average answer

A suitable drug for Sharon to use would be beta-blockers. These act on the heart to calm the person down, and so if she took them she would feel less anxious at times when she was arguing with her ex-husband.

This student has chosen an appropriate drug, so gains 1 mark. There is a little elaboration and the student has tried to apply their understanding of the drug to the stimulus material context. However, the understanding of *how* beta-blockers work, in particular how they would work in this situation, is superficial, so this answer would receive only 1 mark out of the 3 for explanation.

2 out of 4 marks

Strong answer

Beta-blockers act on the sympathetic nervous system and so lower heartbeat and blood pressure, which are characteristics of physiological arousal when a person is stressed. Because Sharon becomes aroused when thinking about or talking about her divorce, this makes her feel anxious. Beta-blockers would lower her levels of arousal, and reduce the impact of this stressor until she is better able to cope with her divorce, at which point it would no longer arouse her and she would no longer need the drugs.

This answer correctly identifies beta-blockers as a suitable drug for treatment. The student explains how they work more clearly and precisely than in the 'Average answer' and with the appropriate detail for the number of marks available. This student has obviously thought about Sharon's particular situation and has applied the knowledge intelligently to that problem. This would receive full marks.

4 out of 4 marks

Part (c)

*Outline **one** limitation of using drugs as a form of stress management.* [**4 marks**]

- It always pays to read questions carefully. In this case, the question asks you for a limitation (not a strength), just one limitation, and of drug treatments generally, i.e. not just a limitation of beta-blockers.
- This is a particularly challenging question, because with 4 marks for just *one* limitation, you would clearly need to elaborate to gain all these available marks.

- One way you could achieve this is to use the three-point rule: *identifying* the limitation (e.g. that drugs only target symptoms), *justifying* it (e.g. providing evidence for the claim that there are side effects), and *elaborating* the limitation (e.g. considering what the implications of these side effects are for the effectiveness of treatment). This would probably give you an answer of roughly 75 words, appropriate for a 4-mark answer.

Average answer

Drug treatments have the problem of side effects. These are consequences that are not intended but may occur when the person takes the drug. Side effects can be very disturbing for the patient.

The student has written this limitation well and accurately *but* needed to elaborate in order to pick up all the marks available. For example, the student might have included some evidence of particular side effects that have been found to be associated with particular drugs. They might also have considered what the implications of these 'disturbing' side effects might be (e.g. the patient may choose not to continue with their treatment).

2 out of 4 marks

Strong answer

A problem for drug treatments is that they can only treat the symptoms (e.g. feelings of anxiety) rather than the underlying cause of the problem. For example, if someone is going through a divorce, drugs can only help them to deal with the anxiety that this creates, it does not help them deal with the underlying problem. This means that the problem will still be there when they stop treatment, and the symptoms will return.

This is a very effective answer that demonstrates the three-point rule. The student has clearly identified the limitation, justified this limitation (i.e. they cannot help them deal with the underlying problem that causes the anxiety) and finally explained why this becomes a problem for the effectiveness of treatment. It would receive full marks.

4 out of 4 marks

Section B: Social psychology

Question 4

Part (a)

Outline what is meant by normative social influence. [3 marks]

- A hierarchy of instructional terms gives you clues about the depth required: *identify* requires very little detail; *outline* and *explain* require a little more, and *describe* requires the most detail.
- The easiest way to find out how much detail is needed, however, is to look at the number of marks available for a question. A 3-mark question like this would require about 50–75 words. The space in the answer booklet also gives you a clue about the appropriate amount of content. Remember not to spend too long on questions that give no extra points for extra effort. You *could* respond in depth to this question, but only 3 marks are available, so find the right balance.

- This question asks for an outline of *normative social influence*, i.e. conformity based on the desire for social approval and the desire to be accepted by other group members. You could elaborate on this by adding that it is usually characterized by public compliance rather than private acceptance, or by stating the conditions under which it is likely to take place.
- You might also elaborate by adding an example to push your answer up to the full 3 marks. Remember, examiners have to discriminate between answers that are worth 1, 2 or 3 marks, so by adding that extra bit of information, you make it easier for them to justify giving you the full 3 marks.

Average answer

Normative social influence is when you go along with the majority because you want them to like you, e.g. doing something you don't want to do because you think people will laugh at you if you don't.

This definition of normative social influence is more or less accurate, though a bit vague, and the example given is appropriate, so the student would receive 2 marks. However, for the final mark the student could have added that the individual may be seeking group approval, or that it is more important when the group is important to the individual, or perhaps that this results in public compliance rather than private acceptance of the majority point of view.

2 out of 3 marks

Strong answer

People conform because of normative social influence when they are motivated by social approval, to be accepted by the majority and not ridiculed by them for being different. This results in public compliance, but may not lead to a change in any underlying attitudes and is more likely when group membership is important to us.

This explanation of normative social influence is clear and precise, and the elaboration appropriate and detailed. An examiner would have no problem distinguishing this answer from one worth only 2 marks. This would get full marks.

3 out of 3 marks

Part (b)

A psychologist is interested in whether people are more likely to conform on a perceptual judgement task when the majority are of the same gender or a different gender.

Identify the independent variable in this study.
[1 mark]

- This question asks you to identify the independent variable in *this* study (the gender of the majority). Answers that simply define what is meant by an independent variable would not gain marks.

Average answer

The independent variable is gender.

This isn't accurate enough for the mark. The student needs to add 'of the majority' because simply stating that the IV is 'gender' is far too vague.

0 marks

Strong answer

The independent variable is the gender of the majority, either the same gender or a different gender to the participant.

Very precise and detailed answer, well worth the mark allocated for this question.

1 mark

Part (c)

Give a non-directional hypothesis for this investigation. **[2 marks]**

- Examiners will expect you to give a precise statement about the predicted relationship between the two variables (level of conformity on the task and whether same-gender or opposite-gender majority).
- Never phrase hypotheses as questions, but as statements of what the researcher believes to be the case.
- As the question asks you for a non-directional hypothesis, you should not state which condition would produce the greater conformity, i.e. you should simply state there will be a difference rather than what you expect the difference to be.

Average answer

There will be a significant difference in conformity between the same sex and opposite sex groups.

This hypothesis is non-directional, and *does* indicate the appropriate relationship between the independent (gender make-up of the majority) and dependent (conformity) variables. However, it is not precise, particularly in the operationalization of the variables, so would not gain both marks.

1 out of 2 marks

Strong answer

There is a difference in the percentage levels of conformity found on the perceptual judgement task between groups where the majority are of the same gender as the participant and when they are of a different gender.

This is far more precise than the 'Average answer'. The student has clearly operationalized the IV and DV. Although the student has to guess the exact way the conformity was assessed, this is perfectly acceptable in an answer. It is appropriately non-directional, therefore would be worth full marks.

2 out of 2 marks

Question 5

Milgram's study of obedience to authority is widely regarded as one of the most influential studies in social psychology. However, it is also one of the most widely criticized.

*Outline **two** criticisms of Milgram's study of obedience.* **[3 marks + 3 marks]**

- The question asks for exactly two criticisms and indicates that 3 marks are available for each. If you only offer one criticism, you can only earn a maximum of 3 marks. If you offer more than two criticisms, the two 'best' ones will be awarded marks – but you will have wasted precious exam time!
- In answering this question, you could outline either positive (e.g. in terms of research support) or negative (e.g. in terms of ethical problems with the research) criticisms of Milgram's study.
- Remember the three-point rule here: identify the criticism; justify it; then elaborate it by explaining why it is good or bad for Milgram's study.
- Be careful not to fall into the trap of presenting false criticisms, for example, criticizing Milgram's study for only using students when, in fact, he did not use students at all; or accusing his study of lacking ecological validity, when it has been replicated with many different populations, with roughly similar results.

Average answer

The first criticism is that the study was unethical and caused people a great deal of psychological harm and stress.

The second criticism is that the study was carried out in a laboratory so doesn't tell us anything about how people would behave in a natural environment. For example, the 'only obeying orders' explanation was not accepted for war criminals after the Holocaust as a relevant explanation of their actions.

The first criticism is appropriate – Diana Baumrind did indeed accuse Milgram of causing his participants psychological harm – but the student does not expand on this. For example, the answer might have identified what it was about Milgram's study that caused the harm, and explained the possible consequences of this. As the student has only identified a criticism, it would be worth just 1 mark.

The second criticism is better, adding an example to justify the point, but elaboration might have included some reference to how this challenges the validity of Milgram's conclusions. This would be worth 2 marks.

1/3 marks + 2/3 marks = 3 out of 6 marks

Strong answer

Baumrind accused Milgram of causing psychological harm to his participants. This is because he put them under considerable stress and also caused them to discover the disturbing fact that they could have killed an innocent person under the orders of an authority figure. Milgram discounted this criticism, pointing out that his participants experienced no lasting harm as a result of their participation in the study.

Mandel (1998) has argued that Milgram's study lacks real world validity. Milgram claimed that the actions of many Nazi war criminals could be explained in terms of their need to obey authority. Mandel claims that this is not supported by actual events, and argues that situational factors such as physical proximity to the victim or an absent authority figure made no difference to those in the killing squads (such as Reserve Police Battalion 101) during the Holocaust.

This answer contains two well-detailed and accurate criticisms of Milgram's study of obedience. They have the same focus as in the 'Average answer' (ethics and real-life validity), but this is much better informed and far more effective. The first criticism, for example, follows the three-point rule outlined earlier: the criticism is *identified* (Milgram caused his participants psychological harm); *justified* (e.g. causing them to realize disturbing truths about themselves) and *elaborated* (Milgram refuted this criticism). Both criticisms would receive full marks.

3/3 marks + 3/3 marks = 6 out of 6 marks

Question 6

Discuss how social influence research helps us to understand social change. [12 marks]

- This is probably one of the most challenging questions that you will come across on this paper. Social change can refer to almost any widespread form of change within a society as a result of social influence. Although this particular question does not tell you which form of social influence to discuss, from 2012 onwards other forms of this question might cite minority influence as the required content. There are several ways that you could approach this question, but minority influence is the most obvious way.

- Description – For the AO1 material, you could describe the 'nuts and bolts' of minority influence. This doesn't mean long descriptions of Moscovici's blue/green slide experiment, but instead concentrating on aspects of influence that have been shown to lead to social change (e.g. drawing attention to an issue, creating conflict, consistency of the minority's message, augmentation).

- Evaluation – For the AO2 material, try to provide actual evidence of social change that might link in to the concepts in the AO1 content. For example, you could use the suffragettes, Gandhi's non-violence movement or even terrorist groups as suitable contexts. However, you must use any inclusions to provide evidence for the AO1 material and not just for their historical interest.

- You also need to bear in mind some general 'structural' requirements when answering this question. There are an equal number of marks for AO1 and for AO2, so split the material 50/50 between the two. Producing AO2 material for this topic is challenging, and many questions will only ask for AO1 content, but this type of question does come up.

- Finally, you will also be assessed on your quality of written communication in this question, so you should write in complete sentences *and* try to use appropriate psychological terms in your answer.

Average answer

Social influence can be seen in minority influence and also in resistance to obedience. Moscovici carried out research that showed that minorities can bring about social change provided that they are consistent. In Moscovici's research groups of women were shown slides that were blue, but two confederates consistently called them as green. This consistency was important, because when the minority was inconsistent, the amount of influence was much less. This has also been found to be the case when societies change. An example of this is the influence brought about by the suffragettes who caused the major social change of women getting the vote. They achieved this by acting consistently over many years. Another characteristic of minority influence is the snowball effect. This happens when a small number of people change their mind and follow the minority. As more and more people change to the minority position, there is a noticeable shift, and the minority then becomes the majority. This is what happened with the suffragettes. To start with a few politicians supported them, and then more and more people changed until the law was eventually changed.

Another finding of minority influence research is that the majority are more likely to be influenced by the ☞

minority if they think that the minority have nothing personal to gain from their beliefs and are actually making sacrifices. Gandhi is a good example of this. He led a group of men on a march to protest against the British Salt tax, and despite the fact they were attacked by troops, did not attempt to defend themselves. This meant that the majority of Indians and the British took their protest seriously and this eventually led to Indian independence.

There is some useful material here, but the student hasn't always used it that effectively.

- Description – For AO1 content, it is okay to mention Moscovici's research, but there is a lot of irrelevant detail for a question that is essentially about social change rather than minority influence itself. The AO1 material is limited and needs more detail, so would probably be worth 3 marks.

- Evaluation – The example of the suffragettes is appropriate, although the student has not developed their inclusion as support for the principles of minority influence. The mention of the snowball effect is also appropriate but not developed. The Gandhi example is slightly better, as the student has effectively ☞

interwoven the principle and the historical example. Overall, the AO2 material lacks development and is not always that effective, and would also be worth 3 marks.

3/6 + 3/6 = 6 out of 12 marks

Strong answer

Research on minority influence has shown that being exposed to the views of a deviant minority creates a conflict in the minds of the majority because it presents a view that contrasts with the established point of view. The impact of the minority position is increased if it is expressed consistently. The relevance of this for social change is demonstrated in the work of the suffragettes. They presented an argument for votes for women that caused a conflict in the minds of the majority. This was expressed consistently through meetings, pamphlets and demonstrations. Minority influence research has also shown that the influence of a minority is strengthened if the minority is seen as suffering to get their point across (the augmentation principle). This suggests that the minority must have great belief in their convictions, so they are taken more seriously. Support for the influence of the augmentation principle also comes from the suffragettes. Historical evidence suggests that much of the influence of the suffragettes came from the fact that they appeared willing to be arrested for their views and even went on hunger strike when in prison.

Kruglanski (2003) claims that terrorism to bring about social change could also be considered a form of minority influence. Terrorists try to bring about social change when direct social force is not possible because they are perceived as a deviant minority. Kruglanski argues that terrorists may accomplish social change by drawing attention to their claims. This creates a conflict in the minds of the majority, and so they are motivated to consider the legitimacy of these claims. Consistency is achieved through propaganda and violence through roadside bombs and the augmentation principle comes from the fact that suicide bombers are willing to die to represent the views of their minority group. ☞

However, if other people are injured during attempts to bring about social change (as was the case with 9/11 and with victims of animal rights violent protests), the minority group loses the moral high ground, and public sympathies switch to the victims than those who commit the violent acts. This would explain why non-violent minorities have traditionally been more successful in bringing about social change than violent minorities such as terrorists.

This student has made a really good job of answering a very difficult question. They have clearly and accurately outlined some of the conclusions from minority influence research most relevant to social change, and systematically applied these to two main examples: the suffragettes and terrorism.

- Description – The AO1 material is mainly in the first paragraph, and is reasonably well detailed, but perhaps needs just a little more detail to gain maximum marks for AO1. It would most probably receive 5 marks for AO1.
- Evaluation – The AO2 material takes each of the conclusions from research and shows how these might be used to explain events in history that have led to (or in the case of terrorism have failed to lead to) social change. The student has introduced these examples as evidence for the application of minority influence principles, and maintains this focus throughout. For example, the augmentation principle is explicitly supported by evidence of suffragettes' hunger strikes and by the actions of suicide bombers. The final paragraph takes the AO2 content past the quality of the AO1 content, and so would receive maximum marks for the AO2 material.

5/6 + 6/6 = 11 out of 12 marks

Section C: Individual differences

Question 7

Two of the following statements apply to systematic desensitization. Tick the **two** *correct boxes.* **[2 marks]**

Pairs an undesirable habit with unpleasant consequences ☐

Individual is taught relaxation techniques ☐

Aims to replace irrational thought processes with more rational and healthy ones ☐

Patients are encouraged to say whatever comes into their mind without censorship ☐

Therapy works on the assumption that two incompatible emotional states cannot exist at the same time ☐

- The correct boxes to tick are the second and fifth boxes. These are the only boxes you should tick. If you were to tick more than two boxes, the examiner would use the first two ticks as your answer.

Average answer

The student ticks all five boxes.

The student obviously doesn't know the answer, so has tried ticking all the boxes and hoping for the best. The examiner would take the first two ticks as the answer and, fortunately for the student, the second one is correct.

1 out of 2 marks

Strong answer

The student ticks the second and fifth boxes.

Both ticks are in the right place, so the student gains both marks.

2 out of 2 marks

Question 8

Michelle displays an excessively pessimistic attitude towards life and has very low self-esteem. She struggles to hold down a job and has problems developing personal relationships.

Part (a)

Identify the definition of abnormality that best describes the characteristics of Michelle's behaviour outlined above. **[1 mark]**

- This question requires the identification of the 'deviation from ideal mental health' definition. All other suggestions, such as other definitions (e.g. failure to function adequately or deviation from ideal mental health), approaches (e.g. cognitive) or specific abnormalities (e.g. depression) would not gain any marks.
- As the question only requires an identification of the correct definition, all you need is just a brief statement of 'deviation from ideal mental health'. You don't even need to put this information into a sentence, or to justify your choice of definition.

Average answer

Michelle shows some of the characteristics associated with the deviation from ideal mental health definition. For example, she has very low self-esteem and has problems with her relationships.

The student correctly identifies the deviation from ideal mental health definition, but has also wasted time providing unnecessary detail justifying this choice.

1 out of 1 mark

Strong answer

Deviation from ideal mental health.

This answer is correct and appropriately concise.

1 out of 1 mark

Part (b)

*Outline **one** form of psychological therapy that might help Michelle and explain why it would be the most appropriate form of therapy for her.* [**3 marks**]

- There is no one right answer for this question as all the therapies covered on the specification could be relevant. What is required is for you to outline your chosen therapy as it might be used in the treatment of this particular set of problems *and* justify why this might be the best form of treatment for the problems Michelle is facing.

- Remember that this is an application question, so you should ensure that you do more than just outline your chosen therapy; you also need to contextualize it within the stimulus material provided.

Average answer

The most appropriate form of treatment would be BZs. These work with the body's own calming chemicals to decrease levels of arousal. These will prevent her becoming anxious and so she would be able to get on better with other people. If she was less anxious, it is also possible that her self-esteem would improve.

BZs may well help Michelle feel less anxious (although we don't know that she *does* feel anxious). The outline of this form of treatment is fairly limited and the justification of *why* BZs would be the most suitable treatment for Michelle is fairly vague, and the student has assumed that anxiety is her main problem (which is debatable), so this answer would not gain all 3 available marks.

2 out of 3 marks

Strong answer

Cognitive behavioural therapy involves a cognitive element, where Michelle would be helped to become aware of the irrational beliefs that have contributed to her low self-esteem. The behavioural element would involve Michelle testing out some of these faulty assumptions against reality through 'homework'. By changing the irrational beliefs that have led to her low self-esteem, she should enjoy more satisfying interactions with others that would in turn resolve her relationship problems.

This answer shows a clear and concise overview of CBT *and* appropriately applies this therapy to Michelle's lack of ideal mental health. The student has engaged with Michelle's particular problems throughout, and has justified why this form of therapy would restore her to a better state of mental health and more satisfying interpersonal relationships. This answer would receive full marks.

3 out of 3 marks

Question 9

The psychodynamic approach to psychopathology has made extensive use of the case study method.

Part (a)

Outline what is meant by the case study method. [**3 marks**]

- The case study method typically involves the in-depth study over time of a single individual or small group and is usually undertaken within a real-life context.

- You could elaborate to make sure you gain 3 marks by mentioning how the case study is used in psychopathological behaviour (e.g. to study the symptoms, reactions to certain stimuli) or by giving details of a particular case study.

Average answer

A case study is where the psychologist studies an individual (e.g. someone who is mentally ill) in detail to build up a very detailed profile of their behaviour.

This answer shows a fairly basic understanding of the case study method. The student is aware that it is individual-focused and that it aims to build a detailed profile of that individual's behaviour. However, this outline is not particularly precise and lacks elaboration, so would just receive 1 mark.

1 out of 3 marks

Strong answer

This is a detailed study of a single individual or group. In order to build up a very detailed profile of the individual or group in question, the researcher uses several different techniques including observation, interviews and psychometric tests. Case studies may involve a representative example of the behaviour in question or an exceptional or unusual case.

This answer is accurate and detailed. The student begins with a simple definition, which gets the first mark available, and then elaborates with the techniques used within the case study method and the different types of case study. This would be worth the full 3 marks.

3 out of 3 marks

Part (b)

*Outline **one** advantage of the case study method in the study of psychopathology.* [**3 marks**]

- This question requires you to think not just ask about an advantage of the case study method, but an advantage of this method *in the study of psychopathology*.

- You could include advantages such as the ability to understand the patterns and causes of contemporary forms of psychopathology, or the ability to determine the most appropriate individual-based form of therapy.

Average answer

An advantage of the case study is that it is an in-depth study of one individual, which would be extremely helpful in studying psychopathological behaviour such as depression or schizophrenia.

This student can't really think of an advantage for case studies in the study of psychopathology, so has given a characteristic of the method and said that this would be useful **in** this area. There is some basic relevance and, as examiners tend to note in such cases, it is better than zero, so does pick up 1 mark.

1 out of 3 marks

Strong answer

The case study method enables psychologists to investigate unusual cases of psychopathological behaviour where individual cases are relatively rare. By studying each of these cases in depth, this means that psychologists can use the insights they have gained to help decide what is the most appropriate form of therapy for each particular individual.

This could be interpreted as two separate advantages (opportunity to investigate rare cases and to determine appropriate therapy), but this student has connected these two points and provided one effective and detailed advantage of case studies *within* the study of psychopathology. Note that implications for treatment are relevant in this context, so this elaboration would gain full marks.

3 out of 3 marks

Question 10

Outline and evaluate the biological approach to psychopathology. **[12 marks]**

- The key features of the biological approach to psychopathology are that disorders have an organic or physical cause, and that mental disorders are related to the physical structure and functioning of the brain. The focus of this approach is on genetics, biochemistry, neuroanatomy, etc.
- The question requires equal amounts of AO1 description and AO2 evaluation.
- Description – For AO1 content, as well as describing *explanations* of psychopathological behaviour, you could also gain marks by describing their implications for treatment.
- Evaluation – For AO2 content, an acceptable way of evaluating the biological approach is by demonstrating that therapies based on its

assumptions (e.g. drug treatments) are effective in reducing the symptoms of a disorder. You could also evaluate the biological approach through research that supports the different causal explanations (e.g. providing evidence to support the genetic explanation of a particular disorder), or perhaps by considering disorders that appear to have no physical cause and can be better explained by other approaches (e.g. those that emphasize environmental or developmental influences).

- You can help make your evaluation obvious by adding 'tags' to the material you intend to be credited as AO2, for example, adding '*This explanation is supported by...*' or '*...which therefore challenges the claim that...*'.

Average answer

The biological approach to psychopathology explains mental disorders in terms of four things. The first of these is brain dysfunction, caused by accident or disease. The second is neurotransmitters, for example people with schizophrenia have low levels of dopamine in their brain. The third is genetics. A lot of mental disorders run in families, so this proves that genetics must be involved. For example, schizophrenia has a strong genetic link because identical twins are more likely to develop schizophrenia than non-identical twins. There are problems for genetic explanations, including the fact that identical twins share a more similar environment than non-identical twins, so this might be the reason why identical twins are more likely to develop schizophrenia. This suggests that environmental factors may be as important, if not more important than genetic factors.

When a mental disorder is diagnosed, a doctor first looks for particular symptoms. For example, in depression, the patient would report things like having a very low mood and not having much interest in doing the sort of things that they used to enjoy doing. The doctor would then identify what mental disorder that they had. For example, they would use DSM to diagnose depression. Because depression is believed to be a consequence of having low levels of the neurotransmitter, they would then decide to treat ☞

the depression by using a drug that raised serotonin levels (such as Prozac). This is one of the main strengths of this approach, because research (e.g. Fava *et al.* 1998) has showed that antidepressant drugs are very effective in treating depression. Some psychologists have criticized this approach to abnormality. Thomas Szasz claimed that mental disorders could not be seen as the same as physical disorders because there was not the same physical evidence. He also claimed that diagnosing somebody as mentally ill because they deviated from social norms was just a form of social control over people that were not accepted by the rest of society.

- Description – The opening to this essay is appropriate, as the student lists some of the constituent explanations of the biological approach. These are accurate and focus the essay on the right type of AO1 content. There is some inaccuracy, as although they are aware that dopamine is implicated in schizophrenia, it is *high* levels rather than *low* levels as they state here. They get some credit however, for making the link between dopamine and schizophrenia. The outline of the genetic explanation of schizophrenia is a little vague, and although the examiner might understand what the student is trying to say concerning twins and the inheritance of schizophrenia, the explanation loses some credit because ☞

it appears to suggest that identical twins are more at risk of developing schizophrenia than are non-identical twins, which is simply not true.

- Evaluation – The second paragraph introduces the aetiology of a typical disorder from the biological perspective. This is creditworthy and sets the scene for the discussion of treatments that may be linked to the biological approach. The student uses the Fava *et al.* study to support the claim of the effectiveness of drug treatments for depression, although they fail to point out that Fava and colleagues found that a very high proportion of patients treated with antidepressants alone relapsed, which casts 👉

some doubt on the validity of this treatment and therefore the biological approach generally. The Szasz claims add a good conclusion to the essay and probably rescues it, providing some much needed AO2 commentary.

3/6 marks + 4/6 marks = 7 out of 12 marks

Average answers: overall

Looking at all the 'Average answers' to Example Paper 2, this set of responses has earned around half the marks available, which is probably enough to earn a Grade C.

Strong answer

The biological approach sees abnormality as an illness or a disease, i.e. it has a physical basis, and like physical illnesses, can be classified and treated by medical means. Abnormal behaviours may be the consequence of low (or high) levels of particular neurotransmitters in the brain. For example, low levels of serotonin in the brain have been shown to be associated with depression. Some people with schizophrenia have enlarged ventricles in the brain, indicating shrinkage of brain tissue. This suggests that abnormalities in the structure of the brain can also cause psychopathological behaviour.

Genetic explanations see psychopathology as the result of genetic inheritance. For example, research has shown that if one identical twin has schizophrenia, the chances of the other twin also developing schizophrenia are 1 in 2, whereas for non-identical twins this figure is about 17%. Each type of twin shares the same environment with their co-twin, so the difference in genetic similarity is the only way to account for that difference in risk for schizophrenia.

A strength of the biological approach is that much of the evidence for the claims of biological explanations can be tested scientifically. For example, there is a great deal of physiological evidence to support the role of neurotransmitters and genetics in psychopathology, which makes the claims more scientifically valid. This also means that it is possible to replicate research, making the results more reliable. A problem for genetic explanations is that the influence of genetics is rarely more than 50%, which suggests that disorders such as schizophrenia are not entirely caused by genetic inheritance.

Biological explanations have also led to the development of effective treatments, for example it is claimed that schizophrenia is caused by excess dopamine activity in the brain. Drugs that reduce this activity have been found to be effective in reducing the symptoms of the disorder. The simplicity of biological explanations of psychopathology is seen as one of this approach's main advantages because it reduces complex behaviour into much simpler physiological explanations. However, many critics argue that a simplistic approach to the explanation of complex behaviours such as schizophrenia is inappropriate because it disregards all the other possible influences, particularly as environmental factors have also been shown to influence the development of ☞

psychopathological behaviour. This also has implications for treatment. Drugs that reduce dopamine activity in the brain do not work for everybody, which suggests that other, non-biochemical factors must be responsible for the development of the disorder. This suggests that treatment on a number of different levels, including the biological level, is necessary for intervention to be effective.

This is an extremely impressive answer. At 430 words, it is also slightly longer than might be expected for a 12-mark answer, but not that unusual. There are individual differences in how much students write throughout the whole paper, and this represents one end of that spectrum. This student obviously knows a great deal about the biological approach although, understandably, has left out some aspects of the approach (e.g. viral infection). This is absolutely fine, as students can decide which aspects of a particular approach best represent that approach for them. However, in order to be able to cover material in appropriate depth, students have to select what to include carefully.

This student has helpfully (for the examiner, and probably also for themselves) divided the material into AO1 (the first half) and AO2 (the second half). This provides a useful visual guide ensuring they have provided equal amounts of AO1 and AO2 material.

- Description – The AO1 material is appropriate, accurate and well detailed throughout.
- Evaluation – The AO2 material is also carefully selected, appropriately elaborated and used very effectively. There is a good balance of depth and breadth in the answer, and the use of specialist terms, and the language generally is of a high standard.

This answer is clearly worth full marks.

6/6 marks + 6/6 marks = 12 out of 12 marks

Strong answers: overall

Looking at all the 'Strong answers' to Example Paper 2, this impressive set of responses would clearly be worth a high Grade A.

Glossary

Agentic shift   Moving from an autonomous state (behaving voluntarily and aware of the consequences of your actions) to an agentic state (seeing yourself acting as the agent of another person and hence not responsible for your actions)

Agonists   Drugs that enhance the action of a neurotransmitter

Androcentric   The tendency of some theories to offer an interpretation of men and women based on an understanding only of the lives of men (i.e. a male-biased perspective)

Antagonists   Drugs that dampen activity by blocking or inhibiting neurotransmitters

Antigens   Substances that the body recognizes as foreign. Harmful antigens stimulate the immune system into producing antibodies that will kill or neutralize the foreign invader

APA   The American Psychological Association (APA), a scientific and professional organization that represents psychologists in the United States

Asch effect   The distortion of an individual's correct judgement by the influence of an incorrect but unanimous opposition

Autonomic nervous system (ANS)   Part of the nervous system that maintains the normal functioning of the body's inner environment. The ANS has two subdivisions: (a) the sympathetic division whose activity mobilizes energy resources and prepares the body for action; (b) the parasympathetic division whose activity tends to conserve the body's energy resources and restore inner calm

Biological determinism   The belief that human behaviours are determined by innate biological characteristics; individual differences in behaviour are therefore attributed to genetic variation rather than influences of environment and learning

BPS   The British Psychological Society, a professional association for academic, clinical, and other chartered psychologists in the UK

Burnout   Physical and mental exhaustion caused by the failure to address sources of stress – in particular, stress in the workplace

Catharsis   In psychoanalysis, the process whereby the expression of an emotion removes its pathological effect, i.e. pent-up emotion (trapped psychic energy) is released as a client recalls and relives a repressed earlier emotional catastrophe, making the psychic energy available for healthy functioning

Classical conditioning   A form of learning where a neutral stimulus is paired with a stimulus that already produces a response, such that, over time, the neutral stimulus also produces that response

Cognitive-behavioural therapy (CBT)   A psychotherapeutic approach that aims to solve problems by altering unwanted patterns of thought and behaviour; it addresses personal beliefs that may result in negative emotional responses, concentrating on understanding behaviour rather than the actual cause of a problem

Collectivist cultures   Cultures that value group loyalty, preferring collective to individual decisions; cultures where the needs of the group outweigh the needs of the individual

Confederate   Someone taking part in a study who has information from the researchers about how to act, i.e. their actions are scripted. The actions of the 'confederate' help to create specific experimental conditions and keep the purpose of the study hidden from the 'naïve' participant

Conformity   The process whereby an individual changes their behaviour or beliefs as a result of real or imagined group pressure

Cover story   In psychological research, intentionally telling the participant(s) something untrue thereby concealing the true purpose of the research

Critical life events   Major life events, such as marriage, divorce, moving house and having a baby, that are scored according to their psychological impact within the Social Readjustment Rating Scale (SRRS) and used to investigate the relationship between life changes and stress-related health breakdown

Cultural bias   A tendency in psychological theory and research to ignore the differences between cultures and impose understanding based on the study of one culture alone

Ecological validity   The extent to which research findings can be generalized to other settings

EEG (Electroencephalography)   A non-invasive technique for recording the brain's spontaneous electrical activity using electrodes fixed to the scalp

Ego   According to psychoanalytic theory, the part of the personality responsible for decision-making and dealing with reality

Ego defence mechanisms   Emergency measures, such as repression, displacement and sublimation, which the ego uses to protect itself from anxiety

Empathetic   The ability to sense and understand another person's emotions

Environmental determinism   The view that much of behaviour is determined by what we learn from living in our natural environment; for behaviourists, the main environmental determinants of behaviour are classical and operant conditioning and social learning

Erotogenic zone   Any part of the body that can become a seat of pleasure – in Freudian terms, especially the genitals, mouth, and anus

External validity   The extent to which findings can be generalized across people (others who were not involved in the original research), places (other contexts beyond the research setting) and times

False consensus effect   The tendency to believe that the majority of group members share similar beliefs to our own

Flooding   A behavioural treatment for phobic disorders in which the person is exposed to a phobic object or situation in a non-graded manner (in contrast to systematic desensitization) with no attempt to reduce prior anxiety and remains there till anxiety decreases

General adaptation syndrome (GAS)   A model, described by Hans Selye, of how the body reacts during stressful situations. There are three stages:
(a) alarm stage, when an arousal response is activated
(b) resistance stage, when the body is apparently coping with the stressor
(c) exhaustion stage – if stress continues for too long, it can lead to physical symptoms such as a stomach ulcer or heart attack

Graded exposure   A behavioural treatment for phobic disorders in which the person is exposed to a phobic object or situation in a hierarchy of feared situations and finds their own way of coping

Hardy personality   Hardiness includes a range of personality characteristics that provide defences against the negative effects of stress: belief that you have control over what happens in your life; commitment (a sense of involvement in the world); challenge (seeing life changes as opportunities rather than threats)

Hormone   A chemical that travels in the blood and controls the actions of other cells or organs

Hypothalamus   An area of the brain lying a little behind the eyes that acts like a thermostat, making sure that bodily functions are maintained within tolerable limits

Id   According to psychoanalytic theory, the part of the personality present at birth; the mental representation of basic biological drives

Information processing approach   The view that the person is a kind of computer and psychopathology is a malfunction in the system

Informational social influence   The process by which a person's attitudes, beliefs or behaviours are modified by the presence or actions of others based on our desire to be right

Insight   In psychoanalysis, an understanding of unconscious reasons for one's maladaptive behaviour

Internal validity   The extent to which a test (or measure) does actually test what it is meant to test (or measure) and the result is not due to an extraneous variable

Learned helplessness   A psychological state produced as a result of being exposed to uncontrollable events; observed in people who give up trying to cope because previous attempts have been frustrated and led to failure

Locus of control (LOC)   Individual differences in people's beliefs and expectations about what controls events in their lives. There are two extremes: (a) internal LOC – the belief that what happens is largely under one's own control; (b) external LOC – the belief that what happens to one is controlled by external factors and agents, such as luck and fate.

Majority influence   A form of social influence, whereby people adopt the behaviour, attitudes and values of the majority members of a group

McCarthyism   Term describing the period in the USA in the 1950s when US Senator Joseph McCarthy led a witch-hunt against people accused of being 'anti-American', usually on the basis of actual or alleged membership of the communist party.

Meta-analysis   A method of combining a number of studies on the same theme in order to detect trends in the behaviour being studied; this technique is often used in systematic reviews

Naïve participant   Someone taking part in a study whose actions are genuine and whose behaviour is the object of study (as opposed to a confederate)

Natural experiment   A type of experiment where the allocation of participants to the different experimental conditions reflects naturally occurring differences in the independent variable (e.g. comparing T cell activity in students before, during and after exams)

Neurotransmitters   Chemical messengers (e.g. serotonin and dopamine) that transmit nerve impulses from one nerve cell to another across the synapse (the gap between neurons)

Normative social influence   The process by which a person's attitudes, beliefs or behaviours are modified by the presence or actions of others based on our desire to be liked or avoid ridicule

Obedience alibi   The term used to challenge the view that by obeying orders, individuals may be excused moral responsibility for their action (as in the case of Nazi guards of concentration camps); this suggestion – a possible conclusion of research into obedience by Milgram – is criticized by Mandel and others who regard it as invalid

Operant conditioning   An explanation of learning that sees the consequences of behaviour as of vital importance to the future appearance of that behaviour. If a behaviour is followed by a desirable consequence, it becomes more frequent; if it is followed by an undesirable consequence or nothing at all, it becomes less frequent

Overdetermined   Behaviour or symptoms having multiple causes

Pathogens   An agent that causes disease, especially a living microorganism such as a bacterium or fungus

Pituitary–adrenal system   The body's mechanism for reacting to chronic stress, focusing on continued energy production

Placebo effect   Any subjective improvement reported by patients who believe themselves to have been given some form of effective treatment but who have, in fact, received some inactive substitute

Progressive muscle relaxation (PMR)   Psychological technique for stress management, working on relaxing the muscles to lower the level of arousal brought about by the stress response (an emotion-focused approach)

Reactive attachment disorder (RAD)   A severe disorder characterized by a child's failure to develop social abilities; may be caused by a number of factors, including child neglect, abuse, abrupt separation from caregivers or frequent changes in caregivers

Reciprocal inhibition   The process whereby two emotional states are in opposition (e.g. panic and calmness) but cannot exist at the same time, with the result that the stronger one prevails (e.g. if calmness has the upper hand – thanks to relaxation techniques – fear must subside)

Snowball effect   Term used to describe the mass movement of members of the majority towards a minority position, after the change of mind of a few members of the majority creates momentum, resulting in more and more people joining the minority

Social change   A major change in the social structure of a society, or some widespread change in the behaviour of individuals making up that society

Social comparison   Looking to others for guidance when we are not sure of the right way to behave, particularly in situations that are novel or ambiguous

Social impact theory   Latané's theory that conforming to social influence depends upon the strength (importance), immediacy (presence) and number of other people in the group

Social influence   The process whereby an individual's attitudes, beliefs or behaviour are modified by the presence or actions of others

Social learning theory   An explanation of the way in which people learn by observing and imitating the behaviour of others, mentally rehearsing the behaviours and then later imitating them in similar situations

Social norms   The rules for behaviour established by a society

Stress inoculation training (SIT)   A cognitive-behavioural strategy used in stress management. It has three phases: (a) conceptualization – client relives stressful event and analyses its features to achieve a more realistic understanding of the demand being made; (b) skills training and practice – to help overcome key elements causing stress; (c) real-life application – putting training to test in real-life situations (a problem-focused approach)

Superego   According to psychoanalytic theory, the moral part of the personality that acts as the conscience

Sympathomedullary pathway   The body's mechanism for reacting to acute stress that seeks to ensure a speedy and efficient response of the body to escape or tackle the situation ('fight or flight')

Symptom substitution   An unconscious psychological process by which a repressed impulse is indirectly manifested through a particular symptom, e.g. anxiety, compulsion, depression, hallucination, obsession.

Syndrome   A cluster of symptoms and behaviours regularly found together in a particular combination

Tolerance   The need to increase the amounts of drug to get mood-modifying effects, risking addiction, when previously the individual would have needed lesser amounts

Type A behaviour   A particular behaviour pattern associated with increased vulnerability to coronary heart disease (CHD). Type A behaviour pattern is characterized by constant time pressure; competitiveness in work and social situations; anger, i.e. being easily frustrated by the efforts of others

Type B behaviour   People with an absence of Type A behaviour; they tend to be more relaxed about events generally, more patient and with a more positive outlook on life, hence having lower levels of stress and a lower associated incidence of CHD

Index